Praise for
The Truth About Search Engine Optimization

"Who knew search engine optimization (SEO) could be funny? With Rebecca Lieb telling the story, it is. Her wry voice is a refreshing and long-overdue translation of 'heavy' technical jargon and concepts such as keyword research, link building, and search engine reputation. Lieb makes SEO accessible, but not so elementary that even experienced professionals will find new things to learn and explore. She presents this complex discipline like the skilled marketer she is, diving in and out of high level views to the nitty-gritty of exactly 'how to' build and maintain a significant search engine presence for websites."

Dana Todd, Chief Marketing Officer, Newsforce,
and Cofounder and Chair of SEMPO

"Rebecca Lieb manages to take the seemingly dry subject of SEO and make it fascinating and easy to understand. Her book instructs exactly how to make a website relevant to both search engines and searchers. Read this, and you will have everything you need to attain the highest possible natural rankings for your site!"

Sarah Fay, Chief Executive Officer,
Aegis Media North America

"In *The Truth About Search Engine Optimization*, Rebecca Lieb does for SEO what she has done for the countless columns she's edited. She cuts through all the myths and nonsense straight through to the fundamental truths. If you need to market online, then I highly recommend you buy this book now."

Bryan Eisenberg, Bestselling Author of *Waiting For Your Cat to Bark*,
Call to Action, and *Always Be Testing*

"It doesn't get any better than this...an experienced journalist demystifies SEO for you. Rebecca Lieb tells the truth about optimizing your website for better visibility in search engines in straightforward English with lively twists of expression that is her hallmark as a writer, editor, and speaker.

Calling on her experience as ClickZ editor and her network of other search engine industry leaders, Lieb teases apart today's SEO complexities for her readers with authority from local to global, in-house to outsourcing, title tags to user-generated content, and what really matters and what does not.

If you've ever found yourself confused by SEO lingo, this is the book for you with advice that is strategic, tactical, and just technical enough for non-geeks.

This book actually tells you what all that SEO jargon—link juice, vertical search, and the hotly debated 'no-follow' tag—really means."

Anne Kennedy, Managing Partner, Beyond Ink,
and Member of Search Engine Strategies Advisory Board

"Rebecca Lieb's book is chapter-by-chapter gold for anyone who needs to understand how we find information on the Web. Once you have the basics and advance into higher-level search knowledge, you can advance your positioning and presence on the Web through search engines."

Kevin M. Ryan, Motivity Marketing, Inc.,
and Chairman of Search Engine Strategies Advisory Board

"The odd thing about the evolving search marketing industry is the huge bandwagon that goes with it. People jump on and regurgitate the same old stuff they heard elsewhere because, to be honest, many just don't get it.

For more than five years, I've been bumping into marketing veteran Rebecca Lieb at search conferences all over the world. And when we meet we talk search—the truth about search.

She gets it!

So, here's my advice: If you're going to buy any book at all on search marketing, make sure it's written by someone who gets it—a book that cuts through the hype and BS out there and gets straight to the meat and potatoes.

Lieb knows the truth about what works and what doesn't. Listen up!"

Mike Grehan, Global KDM Officer,
Acronym Media

"SEO can be difficult to understand, but Rebecca Lieb clearly conveys the many facets of SEO in easy to understand concepts. This book is a great read for people just learning about SEO and those who need to understand the concepts behind SEO."

Ben Lloyd, President,
Amplify Interactive and SEMpdx

"How do you plan, build, and deliver SEO strategies? Read Rebecca Lieb's engaging real SEO truths by the numbers and change your old way of thinking. Learn about SEO, from your own reputation online to new technologies like Flash, AJAX, meta tag development, link building, and long tail strategies for profits and revenue. This is public relations for 2009, and this book delivers!"

Jon Rognerud, Author of
The Ultimate Guide to Search Engine Optimization

"In an industry as diverse and as fast-paced as search engine marketing, knowing which information to act on and which to avoid is extremely crucial. Lucky for us, there is *The Truth About Search Engine Optimization*. In this book, Rebecca Lieb provides a detailed look into the world of SEO and online marketing, all the while exposing many of the truths and misconceptions that exist within our industry. This is a must read for all online marketers."

Karl Ribas, Vice President of Search Marketing,
All Web Promotion, Inc.

"Rebecca Lieb's book covers all you need to know about SEO. Thanks to groundbreaking, exhaustive research and case studies, *The Truth About Search Engine Optimization* will give you hundreds of tips and recommendations to maximize your natural search visibility and improve your conversion rates. It is a must read for anyone concerned about the success of their website. Both beginners as well as SEO practitioners will for sure expand their knowledge after reading this book."

Nadir Garouche, SEO Manager at Gameloft,
and Editor of *SEO Principle*

THE TRUTH ABOUT
ABOUT

SEARCH ENGINE OPTIMIZATION

Rebecca Lieb

© 2009 by Pearson Education, Inc.
Publishing as FT Press
Upper Saddle River, New Jersey 07458

FT Press offers excellent discounts on this book when ordered in quantity for bulk purchases or special sales. For more information, please contact U.S. Corporate and Government Sales, 1-800-382-3419, corpsales@pearsontechgroup.com. For sales outside the U.S., please contact International Sales at international@pearsoned.com.

Company and product names mentioned herein are the trademarks or registered trademarks of their respective owners.

Printed in the United States of America

Second Printing April 2009

ISBN-10: 0-7897-3831-7
ISBN-13: 978-0-7897-3831-8

Pearson Education LTD.
Pearson Education Australia PTY, Limited.
Pearson Education Singapore, Pte. Ltd.
Pearson Education North Asia, Ltd.
Pearson Education Canada, Ltd.
Pearson Educatión de Mexico, S.A. de C.V.
Pearson Education—Japan
Pearson Education Malaysia, Pte. Ltd.

Library of Congress Cataloging-in-Publication Data

Lieb, Rebecca.
  The truth about search engine optimization /Rebecca Lieb. -- 1st ed.
    p. cm.
  ISBN 978-0-7897-3831-8
  1. Web search engines. I. Title.
  TK5105.884.L54 2009
  005.75'8--dc22

                    2008047988

Publisher
Paul Boger

Associate Publisher
Greg Wiegand

Acquisitions Editor
Rick Kughen

Development Editor
Rick Kughen

Technical Editor
Amanda Watlington

Technical Reviewers
Kevin Lee
Amanda Watlington

Marketing Manager
Judi Taylor

Publicist
Lisa Jacobson Brown

Cover and Interior Designs
Stuart Jackman,
Dorling Kindersley

Managing Editor
Kristy Hart

Project Editor
Jovana San Nicolas-Shirley

Copy Editor
Water Crest Publishing, Inc.

Design Manager
Sandra Schroeder

Senior Compositor
Gloria Schurick

Proofreader
San Dee Phillips

Manufacturing Buyer
Dan Uhrig

Part I   The Basics of Search

Part II   The Truth About Being Site-Specific

Part III   Tag, You're It!

Part IV   The Truth About Links

Part V   You Call That a Search Engine?

Part VI   Get a Social Life

Part VII Search Ranking

Part VIII The Truth About SEO Management

Part IX   Don't Be Evil

Part X   Going Beyond

Note: Appendix A is available for free and located online at www.informit.com/title/9780789738318.

Foreword

Rebecca Lieb is a marketing super-maven. I first met Rebecca when she was writing about search, as well as interactive marketing and advertising, as ClickZ's Editor-in-Chief. The company I founded way back in 1996, search engine marketing firm iProspect (sold to Isobar, a division of UK Advertising holding company, Aegis PLC, in 2004), had PR agencies and internal PR teams that worked hard to win her favor in the hopes that she would write about our news. When she was done interviewing me on those occasions when I was fortunate enough to be included as a source, I would always ask her for her take on the news of the day.

Rebecca brings a lifetime of deep marketing experience to her opinions on digital marketing and search marketing. Also, she always had a fresh perspective or an interesting context through which she viewed a particular industry development.

When she told me she would be writing a book about SEO, I was excited for our industry. Books can elevate important ideas to new audiences of important decision makers and expand people's understanding of the priority and importance of an area of study. This book will accomplish exactly that, and I'm certain it will help to elevate the marketplace's understanding of the importance of SEO as the bedrock of search marketing. Though there have been many books written about SEO already, most have been very tactical and dealt exclusively with the particulars of tweaking your HTML or building inbound links. Although Rebecca's book surely contains SEO tactics that can immediately be put into practice to gain higher rankings, her unique perspective as someone immersed in marketing both online and offline ensures that the book speaks to the boardroom or the marketer, and not exclusively to the webmaster.

> [This] book speaks to the boardroom or the marketer, and not exclusively to the webmaster.

This is because Rebecca brings deep marketing experience and a unique historical perspective to every subject she covers. Think about it: Every development at every major search engine over the last several years has been covered by her, or by one of her reporters whose work she reviewed and approved. She was often privy to inside information and advance notice on most important industry developments. Rebecca has chronicled the rise of the Web and of Google, the decline of MSN and Yahoo's market share, and the important developments in our industry.

She has been to almost every industry conference, and enjoyed ringside seats to the rise of digital and the evolution of traditional advertising to a more digital footing. That someone of Rebecca's stature and brainpower has thought it worthwhile to write about SEO is a powerful development, in and of itself, for all of us who make our living working in search.

For years, SEO has been unfairly treated like the ugly stepchild of digital marketing—too complicated and technical for the boardroom or the chief marketing officer. All too often, it has been relegated to the IT professionals to argue about meta tags. PPC search advertising is much sexier than SEO and has lately become the domain of advertising agency types who have greater access to the most senior marketers at major brands.

SEO is the foundation, the bedrock of online marketing.

SEO, or Search Engine Optimization, however, is the foundation, the bedrock of online marketing. It isn't just the foundation of search marketing; I submit to you that it is the foundation of all marketing. This is exactly because we live in a world where increasingly, Google dominates the search landscape, and Google has taught people to love to search.

When people see an ad on TV and they want to learn more, what do they do? They go online and search. When a natural disaster strikes, what do people do? They search. When people have questions about life, about science, about business, about education, about travel, or about their health, what do they do? They search. The behavior of search is becoming an entrenched, and widely adopted, human behavior. We don't even think about it anymore. We just search for anything at all.

In the 12 years or so since search engine marketing has been in existence, we have learned this one truth: All media, all marketing, and all communication have one thing in common—they all drive people to search. And in a recent study conducted by Jupiter Research, of all the people who were stimulated by an offline cause to go online and search, some 40 percent of them actually made a purchase.

And when someone types a keyword into the search box and presses that search button, there are only two possible outcomes:

1. They will find you.
2. They will find your competitor.

Google's market share in the United States is nearing 70 percent of all searches, according to HitWise. Across Western Europe, Google has a 91 percent share of search audience—91 percent!

But Google's dirty little secret is that fully 72 percent of all people who search Google click in the natural or organic search results, not the paid ads. For this reason alone, SEO must be the foundation of your search marketing campaign. If you learn how to cause your website to appear at or near the top of the search results when someone searches for a relevant keyword, you can harvest traffic from Google, free traffic, all day long, month after month—at no incremental cost.

Pay-per-click, or PPC, search advertising has its place, too. It is immediate, and you can control your position and the keywords that trigger your ads to a greater degree than with SEO. But PPC search advertising has significant limitations, too. Every click has a cost. And for most verticals, no marketer can afford to buy every click for all of their keywords. Google will literally throttle your search ad on and off all day long to ensure that you do not exceed your set daily budget. That means that hundreds, sometimes thousands of searchers will never see your ad or know that you exist while searching for various keywords—that is, unless you are also found in the natural search results by using SEO.

SEO ensures that once you attain a top ranking on a particular keyword or group of keywords, every searcher will see your listing— all day long, all night long, every day, week, month, or sometimes even for years at a time.

In this way, every additional ranking you achieve through SEO has incremental value at little, if any, out-of-pocket cost. However, with PPC search advertising, the moment your budget expires so, too, does your visibility. If you run out of money, you are instantly invisible.

To engage in a search marketing strategy that does not first include a foundation of good SEO, which targets the area of the search results page where the vast majority of search engine users click, is like filling your car with gasoline but forgetting to add the oil. It will start right up, but it may not go very far.

And recently, SEO changed dramatically, again. When Google announced "Universal Search," SEO got even more interesting and valuable. No longer were the search results simply "10 blue links," but suddenly search results were colorful with images of videos from YouTube and thumbnails of photographs and news all integrated into the search results. Today, being found at the top of the search results cannot be ensured by merely optimizing your website's HTML. Today, SEO necessarily includes optimizing a variety of different types of media that your company produces, such as video content, PDFs, and photographs. It involves distributing and optimizing each of these forms of media for a variety of different kinds of social media sites and vertical search engines. SEO also means securing listings in the major search engine's "tabs" if you hope to consistently be found on the first page of the search results.

And today, the mass market typical search engines such as Google and Yahoo! are no longer the only ones that matter. YouTube is a search engine of video content, Amazon.com is a search engine of books and products, and Flickr is a search engine of photographs.

Although PPC search advertising can reach into these properties and ensure your ad is displayed alongside this content, SEO strategies can ensure that you are the content being displayed. And remember, search engines are listening to your customers as they discuss and link to your brands in a variety of social media settings, and they're using this information as "signal data" in their relevancy algorithms. Because of this, "social media optimization" now influences your ability to achieve top rankings in the major search engines.

In a world where people search using keywords, and every major website is, to some extent or another, a search engine of specialty content or a source of relevancy information to a major search engine, understanding the concepts of SEO grows in importance every year.

Fredrick Marckini
Chief Global Search Officer, Isobar
Founder and Former CEO of iProspect, Inc.
Boston, Massachusetts

Introduction

Search engine optimization (SEO) is the art and the science of getting a website to appear prominently in organic search engine results when a search submits a query relevant to that website.

In other words, it's about standing out from the crowd. It's being front-and-center when a searcher raises his proverbial hand and says: "Hey! Over here! I've got a question and need an answer. Who's available to help?"

Often, that question relates to "Where can I buy...?" or "Who can I do business with?" A well-optimized website, therefore, is something akin to the Holy Grail of marketing. It provides the right message to the right person at the right time.

And who's the person in question? Well, everyone. Very close to literally everyone, given that the overwhelmingly majority of people in developed countries are online—and searching. Search long ago became the second-largest online activity (after email). Search has evolved from merely providing answers to stated problems and queries. Today, it's the way most people navigate the Web. The major search engines are so good and so fast, search has largely replaced even the necessity of bookmarking favorite online destinations. In recent years, we've even seen the search bar come close to taking the place of the navigation bar in most major web browsers.

Even the most casual searcher has noticed that search is changing. It's becoming deeper, more specific, more personalized, and more customized. Now, searchers can search for (and site owners can optimize for) shopping, blogs, video, images, local resources, books, or audio files. There's almost nothing on the Web that can't be found by, or optimized for, search engines, from the Big Three (Google, Yahoo!, and MSN) to a clutch of highly specialized search engines.

If marketers didn't think being found on search engines was critical to their business strategy, the Big Three would hardly be so big. A company like 10-year-old Google rocketed from obscurity to becoming a multibillion market cap company because marketers are confident that investing in search engine advertising is a wise move. That's why paid search advertising accounted for 41 percent of the $17 billion spent on interactive advertising in 2007. Search is the fastest-growing marketing segment of the Internet, which, in turn, is the fastest-growing channel in the history of media.

The purpose of this book is to introduce you to the basic precepts, principles, strategies, and tactics inherent in search engine optimization. It's about how to make your website "findable" by the right person at the right time.

It's not a book for geeks. It will not teach you how to write code, or get you up to your elbows in programming. But whether you're a small webmaster or a chief marketing officer overseeing a search optimization initiative, you will learn tactics, strategies, and best practices for wrapping your arms around this whole search thing.

If you've got a business with a web presence, not being findable on the major search engines is akin to not being listed in the phonebook—only worse, perhaps.

How can you possibly afford to pass up the opportunity to be there when potential customers or clients come looking for you? At the same time, how can you ensure that they find you for the right queries? Your "steel drums" may be musical instruments, or they may be industrial parts. A properly executed SEO strategy helps you be conspicuously "there" for contextually relevant search queries. The goal, after all, isn't just to attract traffic to a website, but qualified traffic. Both the site owner and the searcher alike benefit from solid SEO.

Finally, a note. Although this book deals with optimizing for all search engines great and small (including some you've likely never heard of), you'll find a preponderance of references to Google, and with good reason. By May 2008, a mind-boggling 71.5 percent of all searches in the United States were conducted on Google (source: Compete). Yahoo! lags far, far behind with 13.3 percent, and the remaining 15 percent or so is splintered between MSN, Ask.com, AOL, and others. If the tactics and practices in this book favor Google as the benchmark of all things search, that's because it is. Google is bigger than the proverbial 500-pound gorilla. In search, it's more like Godzilla. I've, therefore, made an effort not to favor Google in this book, but to present today's market realities that will doubtless hold true far into the foreseeable future—and beyond.

Rebecca Lieb
New York City

TRUTH

Getting noticed by spiders, robots, and crawlers

Spiders, robots, and crawlers are your friends. In the name of search engine optimization, you'll not only learn to love them, but also you'll actually go out of your way to attract them to your site.

In SEO, spiders, robots, and crawlers are more or less synonymous, but don't worry unduly—none have legs or feelers. So, let's consolidate and just use the term *crawler*, shall we? Just bear in mind that you'll sometimes want to attract robots, or lace your site with "spider bait." All belong to the same principle.

So, what's a crawler, and why would I want one on my website, anyway?

A *crawler* is a program or automated script (often called a 'bot, short for robot) that scuttles around the Web visiting URLs. Crawlers navigate from URL to URL by following links on the pages of the websites that they visit.

...you'll sometimes want to attract robots, or lace your site with spider bait.

The major search engines continuously send their crawlers across the vast expanse of the Internet. Crawlers find web pages and copy the text and code on them. They keep these copies in their vast index in a process called *spidering*. This enormous index, which essentially is a database of all the pages on all the websites a search engine crawler can successfully visit, is what the search engines use to provide lightning-fast results when you search. When you enter a search query into a search engine, such as Google, what you're really querying is the search engine's entire index, not the Internet as it exists at that very instant in time.

Of course, web pages change. Sometimes, pages and sites change with great frequency. On top of that, new pages and sites are going up all the time. That's why the crawlers are always out there, visiting and revisiting pages to build, grow, update, and refresh the search engines' indexes.

What's in a search engine's index is what the crawler "sees" when it visits a web page. This vision can differ quite considerably from what a visitor to the page sees. If you want to see what a crawler sees when it looks at a specific web page, visit that page with Internet

Explorer and press Ctrl-A to view the copy (Apple-U on a Mac). Or if you're in Google, click on the Cached link at the bottom of any search result to see the crawler's most recent snapshot of the page.

First and foremost, crawlers are attuned to the words and phrases on each page they crawl. They crawl text and links. When you type a query into a search box, the search engine tries to match your exact search term with the web page most likely to match the words in that search query. In this sense, search engines function in exactly the same way as the opening of Genesis: "In the beginning, there was the word."

Different search engines have their own individual crawlers, and as you might expect, they don't all behave exactly the same way. Some spiders fetch entire pages; others are easily bored and look at only some of the content. Most think the copy in the title of the page and up near the top is more important than what's further down the page. Crawlers can easily hit roadblocks and bail out on entire websites if, for example, there aren't links for them to follow or they come up against the wall of some sort of weird (to them, at least) technology or code. A crawler can also be thwarted if it encounters technology that will trap it so that it cannot easily complete its work.

So, a very significant part of any SEO initiative is to make it as easy as possible for search spiders to find and to crawl your website. If your pages don't get crawled, they won't get indexed by the search engines. If a page isn't in the index, searchers can't find it because as far as the search engine is concerned, it simply doesn't exist. Instead, the searcher will find other web pages, very possibly your competitors'. Links and intelligent site architecture are very much a part of building bridges from individual pages and sections of a website to other sections and pages, effectively paving a clear path for crawlers to follow.

> Some spiders fetch entire pages; others are easily bored and look at only some of the content.

Create a sitemap

One very basic way to help out the search engine crawlers is by creating a sitemap. A *sitemap* is a file (often in XML—Extensible Markup Language) that provides the crawler with a listing of all URLs on the site—at least the ones the site creator wants the crawler to see. Additional information about individual URLs can also be contained in the sitemap, such as when a given page was most recently updated, how often it changes, and how important each URL on the site is relative to the other URLs. (A homepage is usually more important than a "Contact Us" page, for example.)

This information helps search engines crawl the site more intelligently. Google, MSN, Yahoo!, and Ask all accept sitemap submission; however, it should be noted that none guarantee all submitted URLs will be crawled or indexed. (A list of tools for creating sitemaps is in Appendix A, "Resources," located online at www.informit.com/title/9780789738318.)

Sitemaps are particularly useful for websites containing content that cannot be accessed through a browseable interface.

Sitemaps are particularly useful for websites containing content that cannot be accessed through a browseable interface, such as sites that house a large archive or database of information that's only accessible via internal site search. Remember, crawlers follow links, and often such information isn't linked to.

TRUTH

2

Learn to do the Google dance

Until just a few years ago, Google changed its ranking algorithm every month or so. The ranking algorithm is what many SEOs live and die by—it's the complex, top-secret formula that determines how high (or low) a site or web page ranks in organic search results. Is yours the top result on the first page of results, or do you show up as result #24 on the third page?

After all, there's being found, and there's being *found*. The goal of search engine optimization is to rank high in search engine results for relevant queries. Although being #1 generally isn't a realistic or a sustainable goal, you do want to appear on the first page or two of search results. Think of your own search behavior: How often do you venture all the way to page 10 of results for a given query, much less click on a result? Searchers are much more apt to refine their query, and then search and search again.

Although changes to search rankings today aren't as episodic and abrupt as they once were, search engine indexes and rankings change all the time, as well they should.

Pages that no longer exist are dropped from the index. Newly found pages are added. Some pages drop in the rankings; others rise. Every search engine (not just Google) continually tweaks and refines its proprietary algorithms, causing entire websites, as well as individual pages, to almost continually rise and fall in the organic results rankings. Sometimes these changes are subtle; sometimes they're dramatic. They can even be panic-inducing.

> Although changes to search rankings today aren't as episodic and abrupt as they once were, search engine indexes and rankings change all the time....

More than once, I've received frantic e-mail messages from a stressed-out "victim" of changes in search algorithms. Their site "disappeared" from Google or Yahoo!, or dropped down so far in the rankings that it might as well be invisible. "What should I do?" they implore. "How do I get back in? My entire business relies on getting organic search engine traffic!"

Therein lie two critical lessons (maybe we can even call them sub-truths), as follows:

- **#1.** Organic search engine traffic can be so valuable, it can sustain an entire business.

- **#2.** Organic search rankings are something you can work to *influence*, but ultimately you do not *control* them. The search engines' algorithms make that call.

Both are important points to bear in mind regarding SEO. When it comes right down to it, there are no absolute guarantees any page will be listed for free on Google, or on any of the other major search engines.

SEO and public relations

SEO is a lot like public relations in that sense. You can talk to the media, carefully craft your messaging and delivery, send out press releases, and otherwise be present, ready, willing, and able to share information.

Maybe you'll get media coverage, or maybe you won't. Maybe your news will make page 1, or perhaps you'll be buried in a squib on page 62. It's simply not something that's under your control. (Although a highly skilled media relations professional can greatly increase the odds of good placement.)

If you want a guarantee that your message will appear in a newspaper or a magazine the way you want it to and where you want it to be, buy an ad. The content and placement will be entirely under your control. The same is essentially true of search engines—the major ones all sell keyword-based advertising.

> If you want a guarantee that your message will appear in a newspaper or a magazine the way you want it to and where you want it to be, buy an ad.

Advertising versus editorial

There's an essential difference, however, between advertising and editorial, just as there's a difference between appearing in paid search advertising versus the organic results generated by a search. Many companies find value in retaining both advertising and PR in their marketing arsenal. The same holds true when it comes to search.

Most site owners strive to appear in organic results for much the same reason businesses try to generate coverage in the media: It confers legitimacy and boosts sales. Searchers certainly click on the ads that appear in the right column next to organic results. (If they didn't, Google wouldn't be a multibillion dollar company; the company earns its money each time a user clicks on one of those ads.) However, the vast majority of users click on organic results, and express greater confidence in the relevance of those results. In surveys, some users claim to have never clicked on a search ad.

Businesses that pay to advertise on search engines also spend a great deal of time, attention, and money on search engine optimization. They understand this balance of trust and legitimacy. Paid search engine advertising may be a guarantee of placement, but organic results—while often varying in position within the results—can deliver as much (if not significantly more) value on the investment in SEO than the ads do on media spend.

Dealing with rises and falls in site rankings

If you're planning to optimize your site for Google (or Yahoo!, or MSN, or Ask.com)—and if you have a website you want people to find, you should—prepare to do the Google dance. But be prepared for it, rather than let rises and falls in search engine fortunes send you into a tailspin.

Websites rise and fall in search engine rankings and results. They appear, and they even disappear. Sometimes it's clear why this happens; sometimes the reasons are murkier. No search engine is ever going to let the public look under the hood to discover the deep inner secrets of how it really works. That would fling open the gates to abuse its systems, and everyone would lose.

At the end of the day, search engines reward sites with strong, relevant, fresh, frequently updated content, well-structured site architecture, and an intelligent link structure, with strong organic rankings.

Really, it's as simple—and as difficult—as that.

TRUTH

3

It's not about traffic— it's about qualified traffic

Back in the delirious, go-go heyday of Internet Marketing 1.0, in the distant era of the mid-'90s, all that was on the collective minds of marketers, site owners, and web publishers was the giddy notion of "clicks" or "hits." The more, the merrier, or so the thinking went.

More visitors to your website somehow meant you were doing great—even if you weren't making money, or even if those visitors left after viewing just one page on your entire website. Sometimes, they were only visiting because they were promised that if they did, they'd be sent over $20 worth of free stuff at no obligation.

No wonder the next thing that happened was the dot-bomb fallout. Dinosaurs walked the Web. It took the equivalent of a meteor to wipe out a species that, in this case, deserved extinction with all due speed.

We've long since moved beyond just the click as the measure of value on the Internet.

Small wonder, then, that search has become the fastest-growing sector of the Internet, which in itself is the fastest-growing channel in history. Search is about relevance, and above all, about relevant results. When a searcher types "digital camera" into the query box, they do not and should not expect to be delivered a bunch of results pointing to film cameras, or Polaroid cameras, or pinhole cameras, or camera obscura.

They want, and expect, to see relevant results for digital cameras.

There's a tremendous upside to this for anyone who runs a website that has anything to do with digital cameras. That searcher has just raised his hand. He's prequalified himself as someone interested in digital cameras, and is certainly more than open to visiting sites that have content concerning digital cameras. And he wants it now. This digital camera content could be about buying them, selling them, reviews of different digital camera models, news about digital cameras, instructions and tips for using digital cameras, repairing digital cameras—the possibilities are wide open.

If you're running a website that has something to do with digital cameras, that's where SEO comes into the picture. If you were running the only site on the entire Internet about digital cameras, SEO wouldn't be a big deal. It wouldn't even be necessary because your site would be the only "findable" site for that digital camera query. However, with hundreds of billions of sites out there—and more every day—no matter how obscure or arcane your website is, chances are you have more than a healthy amount of competition. Heck, more than 2 million pages in Google's index are about beekeeping.

Without SEO, you're more than likely to be a really tiny needle in a really gigantic haystack.

Without SEO, you're more than likely to be a really tiny needle in a really gigantic haystack. With a well-optimized site, you can capture qualified traffic and come pretty close to the marketing ideal of sending the right message to the right person at the right time: When they raise their hand and say, "Hey! Over here! I need information about beekeeping. Now!" This is what a searcher is effectively doing when he types "beekeeping" into a search query box.

A well-executed SEO plan will help you to capture this qualified traffic—to reach searchers with an expressed interest in what you're offering, or saying, or doing—while at the same time saving you time, effort, and above all, money. SEO can create marketing nirvana: the right message to the right person at the right time.

Yes, there are ways of targeting advertising, particularly online, to reach people potentially interested in those digital cameras or portable beehives. But how can you know if they're really interested in what you've got to say, or sell? Are they trying to learn to take better pictures with a camera they already own? In that case, all those expensive ads touting a specific make or model of camera are likely to be wasted on them. But a well-optimized site has a much better chance of being front-and-center when they're looking to actually buy, or to research, a purchase. At the same time, a poorly optimized site is a proverbial tree falling in the woods when they're searching, but not finding you.

That old joke about the main part of a job notwithstanding, however, there's plenty more to SEO than simply showing up. Search engine optimization involves keeping a number of balls in the air, and constantly tweaking and calibrating them to deliver relevance to the search engines, in order to not only appear on search results pages, but also to appear high enough up in those rankings to be found by a searcher. SEO also means delivering relevance to searchers above and beyond those results, so when they do click and arrive on your website, they quickly find the information they expected to find.

That's because any single one of the billions of other sites on the Web are just a single-click away.

When what's on your site, and the way in which that content is optimized, is relevant to a searcher's query, it's a win-win. The object isn't just to show up in search results, even if that's certainly part of the equation.

Your goal isn't just to get a searcher to click—although that's not chopped liver, either.

Your goal isn't just to get a searcher to click—although that's not chopped liver, either.

The ultimate goal is to meet, if not to exceed, searchers' expectations so that they'll stick around a while, and so that they'll buy, or register, or subscribe, or any of the myriad other potential objectives a site owner might have.

It's, therefore, incumbent on every website owner to ensure that once a searcher clicks on a search engine result and arrives at his site, that the page actually addresses the searcher's need and provides an answer to his query. Ideally, the searcher finds what he or she is looking for on the same page that shows up in the search result.

This is why many businesses develop content strategies around their offerings. A digital camera merchant, for example, might provide buying guides, or articles about different types of digital cameras and what various technical specifications mean or cost. This not only increases the likelihood of appearing in the search results for a variety of queries around the term "digital camera," but also ensures the site addresses the searchers need on a variety of levels beyond merely "click here to buy."

TRUTH

4

Your reputation is on the line

When you really think about organic search and how it works, you'll find it's a lot like public relations. (In fact, SEO can play an enormous role in a PR strategy, which we'll examine in Truth 22, "Using SEO PR as a link strategy"). SEO isn't advertising. In advertising, you buy broadcast or print or outdoor media, and then get to put pretty much whatever you want in that space or time for as long as you want—or can afford.

Organic search is different. The pages that appear in organic search results are the pages the search engine's algorithms think belongs there. Like issuing a press release or speaking with the media, you put information "out there" and hope for the best. To be sure, you can influence what's out there. You can put a positive spin on it, emphasizing some points, while de-emphasizing others.

But at the end of the day, what appears in the search results—not unlike what appears on the evening news or in the morning paper—isn't solely determined by you. Search engine algorithms make the call.

Heaven knows, you're not the only one out there clamoring for attention—so are your competitors. And so, unfortunately, your detractors are vying for the same attention. SEOs often recommend a simple test: Conduct a query on your company name, or the names of your brands or products, names of your management team, accompanied by the qualifier "sucks." Too often, businesspeople are utterly shocked and horrified at what shows up in organic search results, not to mention being at a complete loss when it comes to coming up with a strategy to actually combat those negative results.

If not for forever, organic search results can live on for a really, really, really long time. Take the case of the Kryptonite lock. Several years ago, a guy named Chris Brennan discovered that you could easily open one of these expensive, top-selling bicycle locks with a few twists of a cheap and ubiquitous Bic pen. Brennan posted a couple of how-to videos on the Web. And boom—the discovery turned into a viral phenomenon, a high-profile news story, and unsurprisingly, a PR catastrophe for Kryptonite.

Fast-forward four or five years, and search on Google for "kryptonite lock." The first two results are for the manufacturer's websites. But the #3 result—way up high on the page—is a *Wired* magazine story entitled, "Twist a Pen, Open a Lock," dated

September 17, 2004. The next result is an entry on the super-popular blog, Engadget, from a few days earlier, with the headline "Kryptonite Evolution 2000 U-Lock hacked by a Bic pen—Engadget." YouTube videos of the foiled locks are featured. A number of articles harshly criticizing Kryptonite's response to the revelation are next in the search results. There are links to audio files, such as a radio show segment that asks: "Can Plastic Pen Defeat Kryptonite Bike Lock?"

You get the idea. The company tripped up. Back in September 2004, Kryptonite was subjected to a PR fallout.

On the Internet, as far as Kryptonite is concerned, the fallout is still falling, regardless of the fact that nearly five years have elapsed since the crisis. As far as anyone searching "kryptonite lock" is concerned, Bic pens are opening Kryptonite locks in the here and now. That's because the overwhelming number of page 1 search results for "kryptonite lock" refer not to the company, not to the product, not to information about bike security, testimonials from satisfied users, reviews of the products, new company or product announcements, or retail results. Search "kryptonite lock," and you'll get all Bic pen, almost all the time.

Yikes!

Whose fault is that? After all, the term "Dell Hell" no longer appears on the first page of results when you search the computer manufacturer—although it did, and remained there for a long, long time, after Dell incurred the wrath of A-list blogger Jeff Jarvis in the fall of 2004, at pretty much exactly the same time the Kryptonite storm unleashed its fury. In fact, today the first page of Google results for a search on "Dell" contains only one negative result. And it's quite far down the page, well "below the fold."

That search results are dominated by negatives for Kryptonite and relative positives or neutrals for Dell is no accident. It's not that the search results are more or less relevant for either company or brand. In both Kryptonite's and Dell's case, the results are very relevant. Yet there's certainly no confusing which set of search results you'd rather have show up on a search for your company, product, or brand name.

It is no accident that Dell managed to wipe the lion's share of negative results from the first page of search results. Dell had more negative web content created about it than Kryptonite ever generated with the Bic pen debacle. But Dell paid attention. It changed its practices as a result of the Dell Hell fallout and instigated a significant push to respond to media, bloggers, and its own customers about what it was doing to be a better company.

Dell created new web content. It took action, and those actions prompted untold legions of others to create new Dell-related content on the Web. This new content relates to its products, practices, and successes rather than its failings. Over time, the weight (or is buoyancy a better term?) of this new, positive, and better content took its toll. Bit by bit, result by result, the positive feedback rose higher and higher in organic search results. Although there are few absolute truths in SEO, there are some. One of those truths is when something rises in rank, something else will have to fall. There simply cannot be two #1 results.

SEO may not have been the central goal of Dell's crisis management PR strategy, but you can be sure SEO was certainly a core goal of the campaign. Although what dogged Kryptonite five odd years ago remains front-and-center, Dell's problems remain, relatively speaking, largely consigned to the archives.

Search results are not something you can control. But if you're smart, and if you know what you're doing, you can wield plenty of influence over what shows up in them—and even over what doesn't.

Search results are not something you can control. But if you're smart, and if you know what you're doing, you can wield plenty of influence over what shows up in them.

It all boils down to one simple rule: Fight content with content. Although you can't remove the negative, you can accentuate the positive. Although you can't rewrite yesterday's news, you can develop a plan to create newer, fresher, more relevant, and more recent content over time. There's no quick fix for eradicating negative search results, but over time, "bad" results can be pushed farther and farther down the search engine results page as it's superseded by relevant and fresher results.

TRUTH

5

SEO is an ongoing project, not set-it-and-forget-it

The site is optimized! Can you go home now? Not on your life. For better or for worse, search engine optimization has a beginning, but it doesn't have an end. Search doesn't sleep, so neither can search optimization.

SEO begins with determining what keywords and phrases will help your site be found via search engines and optimizing accordingly (more on keywords later in this section). SEO is about site design and management, the technology platforms upon which the site is built, the content and the copy on the pages, and the architecture and hierarchy of that information. It's about making the site easily "crawlable" by search engine spiders. It's about having strong links, both inbound and outbound, to other relevant sites on the Internet (more on links in Part IV, "The Truth About Links").

> For better or for worse, search engine optimization has a beginning, but it doesn't have an end.

The Web is a moving target

You can get all these parts right, but that doesn't mean they'll stay right. Search is continually evolving. If a search optimization strategy doesn't continue to evolve and reassess itself, a site can become unoptimized faster than Yahoo! or Google can deliver search results.

Remember the term *brochureware*? It refers back to the early days of the Web when businesses would translate a corporate brochure, sales sheets, annual statements, executive officer biographies, and contact information onto a website. Brochureware sites were intended to be permanent. They were static.

Websites must now be ever-growing, changing, and evolving platforms for publishing content, news, and information about products and services. They must continually add (and delete) information that's new or no longer relevant. These days, websites often feature images and rich media, such as audio and video. Often, new content, copy, features, and sections are added by different stakeholders in an organization: marketing, PR, sales, perhaps a community manager, or even the site's own users and visitors. Websites no longer change from year to year. These days, they can frequently change and be updated minute-by-minute.

Your own website isn't the only thing changing, of course. Your competitors' sites, which use the same keywords and phrases you're using, are changing, too. New sites are entering into the fray.

As the user-generated Web 2.0 revolution takes hold, much of this new content might be appearing on social media sites, some of which is beginning to get somewhat preferential treatment by the search engines. Over the past year or so, for example, Wikipedia entries have begun showing up high in Google's results.

As you'll recall from Truth 4, "Your reputation is on the line," when something suddenly ranks higher on an organic results page, it usurps the position of the previous occupant of that slot, pushing other highly ranked results a bit lower on the page. A few rounds of that frequent phenomenon can cause highly ranked sites and pages to all but disappear from the first few pages of the search results. And precious few searchers have the tenacity to scan organic search results beyond the second page.

Search engines change, too

Websites, of course, aren't the only moving target. As discussed in Truth 2, "Learn to do the Google dance," search engines themselves are changing all the time. They change how they crawl and index sites. They change their system for ranking sites higher (and lower) in search results. And as mentioned previously, they may suddenly and without warning decide to give somewhat preferential treatment to a Wikipedia, or another specific site or genre of sites. This, in turn, affects all the other sites ranking for that specific query. A new breed of "social" search engines require human intervention for content to rank, rather than relying solely on objectively functioning algorithms.

Search engines are introducing new features all the time. This alone makes SEO even more of a moving target. With increasing frequency, it's not just your average, run-of-the-mill web pages that show up in organic results. The Big Three search engines are pushing new products and features such as local search, video search, image search, blog search, product search, book search, and news search to their users. The past year or so has ushered in a flurry of "blended" or "universal" search results in organic results (see Truth 33, "Universal

19

search and personalized search," for more on universal search). The result is that SEO projects have suddenly had to take all these different search channels into account in a big way. Not only are images from videos and news stories appearing on a search for, say, "Madonna," but these results from different search channels also are pushing "regular" search results—good, old-fashioned web pages— further down (or even off) the page.

Even the fact that search engines are featuring these new types of content in organic results has resulted in new SEO challenges— namely, optimizing all these different types of web content. A small business (say a dentist or a dry cleaner) may need to appear in local search results more than it would in general web results. That headline or press release, whether positive or negative, could be one of the first things a searcher sees. Suddenly, you may be noticing that an improperly tagged product shot or executive portrait doesn't appear when and where it should.

SEO SOS!

Search never sleeps. So neither can the tactics or the strategy of search engine optimization. To keep a site from dropping in the rankings, pay heed to the following critical elements:

■ Develop a content strategy to keep sites fresh, relevant, and attractive to spiders.

■ Keep an eye on the keywords searchers use to find you. (They're in your web analytics tool.) Watch for trends in the words and phrases used to find your site, and create relevant content and pages that address those needs.

■ Pay attention to new products and services the major search engines roll out. How can your site or business benefit from local search? From mobile search? From shopping search? Map search? Not all these features are relevant to every site, but the right search channel can open up a broad avenue of new opportunities for your business.

TRUTH

6

SEO is not an afterthought

Not long ago, I did a favor for a friend and paid a visit to the U.S. corporate offices of one of the world's top luxury brands. Despite being a global household name, the company had never sold directly to consumers. But an ambitious, lavishly produced, and expensive new website intended to change all that. With the site close to launch, together with a splashy (and pricey) ad campaign, the concept of search engine optimization suddenly blipped on the company's radar screen.

How well did I think the site was going to do in terms of showing up in search engine results? That's what this executive, showing off many months of hard work, wanted to know.

"Please don't shoot the messenger," flashed through my mind just before I broke the bad news. The site was not only not going to do well with the search engines, but it was not even going to show up in the search engines. As far as Google, Yahoo!, and MSN were concerned, this meticulously conceived, spare-no-expense production of a website wasn't going to exist any more after its launch than it did before it was even on the drawing board.

That's because the entire site was built in Flash.

Without a significant amount of technical expertise, both in SEO as well as in web coding and development, Flash simply doesn't exist insofar as search engines are concerned. When a search engine spider finds and crawls a web page built in Flash, just about all it sees is the name of the page (assuming, of course, someone remembered to name the page).

> When a search engine spider finds and crawls a web page built in Flash, just about all it sees is the name of the page (assuming, of course, someone remembered to name the page).

The time is now

When it comes to website design, or to redesigning an existing site, the time to bring in SEO expertise is sooner, not later. You wouldn't have an architect complete blueprints for a new house, and then suddenly decide perhaps electricity or plumbing should be part of the project. The same thing applies to SEO. Sure, you can always rip down a wall or swap the places of the bedroom and the upstairs bath once they've been constructed—but why put yourself through the agony, expense, and hassle?

Conversely, why would a website's capability to be found by search engines be an afterthought rather than a fundamental element of the planning process?

One of the biggest mistakes in online marketing—not just in search engine optimization—is this "build it now/worry about it later" attitude toward the searchability and findability of websites. Just as you'd need to know if you're constructing a log cabin or an igloo before hiring an architect, you need to make search a priority that influences every single aspect of online design and development.

To avoid costly mistakes, not to mention the hassle of undoing or redoing weeks of hard work, SEO considerations should be part of any website project from the beginning. The person responsible for SEO should meet with the designer(s), developer(s), and copy-writer(s) to ensure that navigation, code, text, URL structure, tags, page structure, redirects, and a host of other site elements are addressed.

None of this should indicate that SEO can't help an already-extant website, of course. It can, and as discussed in the last truth, SEO is an integral part of the ongoing maintenance of any website that wants to be found on the Internet. But in an age when performance and achieving business goals are critical to the success of many sites, why would anyone in his or her right mind not seize the opportunity to bake "findability" into a website from the get-go?

Conducting initial keyword research will help determine what keyword queries the site must target. Doing so is not only essential to SEO, but it also will help to determine what type of site is required. This early planning will help shape the information architecture of the entire website, even down to the number of pages required to give each set of keywords their due. Because keywords must be surrounded by targeted, relevant copy, SEO is going to determine what words are on the site's pages to start with. It will influence the design, development, and coding of the site's pages. And as we saw in the previous illustration, SEO concerns are going to influence the technology platform on which your site is built.

23

The time to start worrying about SEO is always now. SEO concerns and considerations must be raised before a site is speced out, during the development, design, and build processes, as well as after launch.

TRUTH

7

SEO results aren't immediate or lasting

Good, solid SEO requires investments on several levels. As discussed in the previous truth, it's best to consider SEO during all phases of site design and development. Of course, SEO requires a good deal of thought and often, a financial investment in the necessary expertise. That doesn't mean, however, that there will be an immediate payoff of solid, targeted traffic to your website.

Organic search optimization is a process that evolves over time. There are no instant payoffs. Patience is paramount for long-term success. So, let's examine some of the hurry-up-and-wait aspects of organic search.

Choosing the right keywords and phrases

Even the search-friendliest sites can't control when, how often, or how deeply they're crawled and indexed by search engine spiders. That part is up to the search engines. Merely being found, however, isn't the goal. A well-optimized website will not only be found, but will also rank high in organic search results for relevant, targeted keywords and phrases—the very same words and phrases searchers use in making queries. Often, a site may show up in search results, but not rank well until its keywords and phrases are fine-tuned to reflect the language searchers use when they're looking for you. This can vary considerably from the language you use (more about this in Part III, "Tag, You're It!").

Establishing a solid link strategy

Another time-intensive element of SEO is creating and implementing a solid link strategy (which we'll go into in depth in Part III). It's not only about your site linking out to other places on the Web; it's also about getting as many relevant and authoritative sites to link to yours as possible. Because you don't control what other sites do, this, too, requires an investment in time and resources.

Links are critical not only to how search engine spiders find your site, but also in terms of how highly a site is ranked by search engines. Remember, spiders navigate by "crawling" the Web from link to link, so more links pointing to your site makes it that much easier to find. High rankings are determined not by relevance alone, but by the quantity and, above all, the quality of sites linking to your own. Developing high-quality inbound links isn't something that happens overnight.

Well, perhaps it is. But the odds that you're going to get a solid gold link from a site as authoritative as *The New York Times*, or a blog as widely-read as boingboing.net, are like hitting the jackpot. It could happen, but don't hold your breath.

High rankings are determined not by relevance alone, but by the quantity and, above all, the quality of sites linking to your own.

Put your money where your site is

Looking for shortcuts? You could consider paid inclusion in the search engine index, once offered by a number of search directories, but now only available from Yahoo! among the major search players. For an annual fee, Yahoo!'s Search Submit Basic program promises an express human review of the submitted URLs for inclusion in its search index within four days. You pay upfront, and although inclusion isn't guaranteed, it's pretty much assured for sites not violating Yahoo!'s policy guidelines. The approved URLs remain in the index so long as the fee is paid, and Yahoo! promises to regularly crawl those pages.

Paying for placement is great, but you're probably counting on being found on Google, too. Google has close to an 80 percent share of all searches conducted on the Web. And you don't pay Google to get into its index. You do your best, and wait for them to find you.

Need a quick fix? Is it critical your site shows up in search results today? It can happen.

Often, websites do have short-term visibility needs. A sale or promotion is one example. Perhaps your organization needs public visibility in the short term related to news, current events, or a holiday. In such cases, SEO is not a viable option.

SEO versus buying an ad

There's only one really viable alternative to guarantee you'll appear on a search results page for a specific word or term: Buy an ad.

Like public relations, SEO is a long-term process. It offers very tangible benefits and rewards. There's a level of credibility inherent in appearing in organic, as opposed to paid, search results that marketers and consumers alike understand and appreciate. It's not unlike a mention in the objective editorial section of a newspaper or magazine.

Good, solid SEO can heavily and positively influence how and where you appear in search results. But influence isn't the same thing as control, which is why organic search optimization is frequently combined with paid search, as well as all the other tools in a marketer's arsenal.

SEO requires a long-term strategy and an ongoing commitment to deliver long-term—but rarely immediate—benefits. Recently, I launched a new site, and to my surprise and delight, it showed up on the first page of Google's results for my top keyword within 72 hours.

I was delighted. But I also considered myself lucky. I would have worried if four weeks had gone by with no results, but three days was pretty darn good!

Sure, I can pat myself on the back and congratulate myself for knowing a thing or two about search. And yes, the site was optimized. But at the same time, I know a few things about search engine algorithms and spiders.

So thanks, Google, for getting my site into the index so quickly. (Weeks later, it's even risen a bit in the rankings.) I may have done the SEO part, but in this case, I also know where the credit is due.

While you're waiting for spiders to visit, and revisit, your site, make sure the house is in order by continually doing the following:

- Monitoring the keywords and phrases searchers use to find you and ensuring that the site contains plenty of relevant content.

- Adding new outbound links, encouraging inbound links, and periodically checking existing links to make sure they still direct to the page to which they are supposed to point.

- Consider paying for placement in major indexes and directories to increase the odds those spiders will find you.

TRUTH

8

You don't have a homepage anymore

Once upon a time, websites had homepages. Homepages nearly always existed at the top of the domain structure. They resided at an URL that looked something like this: *www.OurCompanysName.com*. Homepages were considered the entry points of websites, functioning pretty much the same way as the lobby of a building does. Visitors are expected to walk through the front door, look at the directory, and perhaps even sign in. Only then could they proceed to their intended destination, be it the correct floor, apartment, or even a single room in the complex.

Search has changed all that. Thanks to search results for specific keyword queries, visitors now stream into websites via side doors and back doors. They magically teleport to the basement or the roof without so much as passing Go (or passing through that once all-important lobby). They're practically flying through the windows to land directly where they want to be.

Effective search engine optimization is changing the website paradigm even more. Certainly, websites continue to have homepages, but homepages hardly function as the gateways they were before search became the primary method through which users navigate the Internet.

Say, for example, you're searching for an Apple iPod. The first organic result the search engines display isn't www.Apple.com. Instead, it's deeper in the site: www.Apple.com/iTunes.

What's the lesson here? Any and every page on a website that appears in search engine results is a potential landing page for searchers. By extension, this means that each landing page is the potential gateway for that entire website. Poof! Every single page on a website that search engines know about is now a homepage.

> Any and every page on a website that appears in search engine results is a potential landing page for searchers.

For the searcher, this is extremely convenient. It helps them to quickly find and directly navigate to the relevant results they seek. There's often no need to scan a site's navigation, to burrow down through categories and subcategories of content, or to use the site's own internal search mechanism.

For site owners and operators, there are other implications to this. When every page is a homepage, the importance of optimizing each and every individual page you'd potentially want a searcher to visit is magnified. When visitors can enter a site and land anywhere, there are brand implications as well. If it's not immediately apparent where they are, and why, they might not stick around.

If there's a perception that they've landed on the wrong page of a site that looks promising, it must be immediately apparent what to do next. Is there clear site navigation on each page? An internal search box? Information indicating what site section they landed on? Does the page clearly indicate the name of the site and contain other information that anchors it back to a brand and/or a domain? If they landed on a product page but the product isn't exactly right, is there a "more like this" button, or a listing of comparable products?

Just as searchers are looking for relevant results, website owners who hope to be found in search engine results have goals: a sale, a sign-up, a subscription, or some other type of conversion activity. If the site's goal is to get visitors to sign up for a free newsletter subscription, for example, make sure that call-to-action exists on every page of the website.

Gone are the days when a website's homepage could be counted on to do the heavy lifting. Now, all search-findable pages must be counted upon to do the lifting all by themselves. When searchers search, they find the page that matches their query. Search the title or author of a specific book, for example, and you're going to get results for the page that sells that book or that author on Amazon.com or BN.com. Click on one of those results, and you'll land directly on the relevant page.

For this reason, page titles, descriptions, and tags, as well as the actual copy and other content that appears on a given page, must match up with the searcher's expectations when he or she clicks on a search result. Even the navigational hierarchy matters to some extent. A searcher can make sense of that earlier example: www.apple.com/iTunes. There's an implicit iPod in that URL structure, even if it doesn't explicitly say so. The page is titled "Apple - iPod + iTunes." The page description, visible in search results, begins, "Learn about iPod." Product photos are front-and-center, as is Apple's branding. You know you're in the right place. You know it's Apple's place. In a sense, it could be considered a homepage, not for the product's manufacturer, but for the product itself. It displays all flavors of iPod: the Touch, the Shuffle, the Classic, and the Nano (each of which has its own landing [or home] page, of course).

The lesson here? Search engines enable searchers to cut to the chase. This fact should direct your site's development, structure, copy, and keyword strategy. Don't count on wooing them with lengthy introductions or an exchange of pleasantries. Instead, be ready for them when they get to your site.

TRUTH

9

Think like a publisher, even if you're not

Every website, whether personal, business, informational, a blog, or even an online store, publishes information. By default, that makes every website owner and operator a publisher, whether they think of themselves that way.

To optimize a site for organic search, you'd do well to think of yourself as a publisher—starting now. You might as well, because if you have a website, you're publishing information about something: your business, your products and services, your passion for fly-fishing, favorite recipes, something. Unless you're interested in sharing that information with the Internet community at large rather than just family and friends, you ought to be thinking strategically about your website's content.

Good, strong, relevant content—and above all, good writing—is a powerful differentiator, and one that over time tends to be rewarded with higher placement in search engine rankings.

So what is good content?

- Good content is well-written. It contains few (better yet, no) spelling or grammar mistakes.

- Much like a newspaper or magazine, it is updated frequently and presented in short, easy to digest paragraphs rather than in long, rambling blocks of text.

- The keywords or phrases searchers use to find you should be included in the writing, ideally higher up on the page. If a website's purpose is to sell beekeeping supplies, terms such as "beekeeping," "bees," and perhaps "honey," "honeycomb," "net," and "hive" belong in the information on that site's pages. (A discussion of how to research keywords and phrases is included in Truth 12, "Keywords are key.")

> **The keywords or phrases searchers use to find you should be included in the writing, ideally higher up on the page.**

Develop a plan for updating content on a regular basis. Daily would be great, but weekly or monthly work well, too. Develop content with a narrow, targeted focus. The purpose of website content is to educate, inform, and enlighten visitors, as well as to provide search engine crawlers with a clear and focused notion of what it is your site is trying to sell or to accomplish. If you can't write, it's worthwhile to consider paying someone who can.

Bear in mind that all-important search optimization adage: "In the beginning, there was the word." Above all else, search engines are concerned with one thing: text. The words on each page of a site are what the search engine matches to queries. The closer the match, the greater likelihood there is of that page being relevant to a search query.

There are creative ways to bring relevant content into a website that don't burden the site owner with the onus of writing it all from scratch. Customer reviews are one such example. A recent study by PowerReviews and The E-tailing Group reports nearly 9 out of 10 U.S. buyers read customer reviews at least "some of the time" before buying.

Additional content examples might include company press releases (you do post these on your website, don't you?), white papers, news articles (used with permission), case studies, how-to's and user tips for products and services, and research reports.

This type of content affords benefits that go beyond supplying search engines with relevant text and copy. Strong content induces repeat visits to a site, and just as importantly, provides reasons for external sites to link to your own. Links, as we've seen, make it easier for crawlers to find your site and (as we'll examine in Truth 20, "Some links are more equal than others") are a major criterion used by search engines when determining how high a site will rank in organic search results.

Retailers and service providers are advised to consider all aspects of the sales cycle when developing content strategies. Let's use plastic surgery, a high-consideration purchase with a fairly long and educational sales cycle, as an example. The American Society of Plastic Surgeons gets it right. The first line of copy of the relevant page reads, "Also known as rhinoplasty, nose surgery...." Right off the bat, they're paying attention to the keywords a searcher might use to find the page (rhinoplasty and nose surgery). The page goes on to outline initial considerations, the different types of surgery, finding a physician, what to expect in the consultation, costs, what to expect from surgery, recovery, long-term results, prescriptions, health tests, a list of "words to know," and more. This one page covers the waterfront in terms of the entire rhinoplasty sales cycle, and addresses every possible question a prospective patient (buyer) might have. Small wonder the page resides as the #1 search result for a term that's not even included in any copy on the page: "nose job." That's the SEO reward for clear, informative, and educational content.

This is also where thinking like a publisher comes in. Most businesspeople are too close to their products or services to break them down into these small bite-sized nuggets of information. Plastic surgery might be a high-consideration purchase, but search is used as a research tool for all kinds of transactions. If you sell something utterly utilitarian and straightforward, such as nails, don't despair. Get to thinking. Create informative, compelling content describing the different types of nails: What nails are used for what jobs? Which nails are better for construction, and which are better for crafts? Describe the difference between stainless steel, galvanized, and copper nails. Explain why the length and type of head matter. Create a how-to section on choosing the right nail for the job.

There's probably more, but I don't know the first thing about nails—but I do know the type of questions that I might be asking if I were planning to buy nails for a project. If you sell nails, you know what questions your own customers ask before buying. A good content strategy begins by tackling those questions head on.

TRUTH

10

Site and page design count

An oft-repeated SEO truism: "Search engines like big, dumb, ugly pages." If they had their druthers, search engines would very likely subsist on a diet of plain text.

Website design issues can affect search engine ranking, particularly elements such as splash pages, frames, and dynamic delivery. That doesn't necessarily mean you shouldn't use these design elements, or other design bells and whistles. The Web would be a stark, boring place if all you saw on web pages were words. It's also important—nay, critical—to bear in mind that first and foremost and above all, every website should first be designed and conceived with the end user in mind, not the search engine.

Buying furniture is a good analogy. It's all well and good to find the most comfortable, thus user-friendly, armchair in the world. But you also want it to match the rest of your living room's décor—a pleasing environment is friendly and welcoming, too. As with decorating, site design is about style and comfort. It's about satisfying visitors, while at the same time keeping a door open to search engine spiders.

The goal of many websites is to get users to convert, or to take some sort of desired action. So, although I may tell you that Google and Yahoo! don't particularly care if you have that lush product shot on the page (and really, they don't care a lot), that same photo will be a critical part of getting the visitor who's on the page (perhaps she arrived via a Web search) to decide to click and purchase the compelling product depicted in that photo.

Design do's and don'ts

When all is said and done, a user-friendly website is a search engine-friendly website. (Unless, of course, Google, Yahoo!, Ask, and MSN are your prospective customers. If that's the case, go ahead. Design for search engines.) Therefore, the following list shouldn't be considered hard-and-fast rules of website design. They're suggestions. If you elect to "break" one of these rules, compromise by compensating in another area. Use good judgment, and above all, conduct usability tests to ensure that the design and structural element of the website are at least as pleasing to users as they are to search engines, if not more so. Here are the rules:

- **Avoid splash pages**—Splash pages, which appear briefly as introductory website home pages, tend to be graphic-heavy and text-light. Most splash pages link to only a single page within a site. This format tells the search engine crawlers that only one page on your site is of any importance.

- **Avoid frames and inline frames (iframes)**—Frames and inline frames make it difficult for search engines to crawl websites because they break each page into three or more files, rather than just one files, which is standard. These files link to one another in a way search engine spiders can't follow.

- **Be careful with drop-down navigation menus**—Use search-friendly cascading style sheets (CSS) to build drop-down menus, and avoid JavaScript DHTML. If a menu is built with JavaScript, be sure to include a secondary, text-based navigation, because again, JavaScript links aren't navigable by search engine spiders.

- **Define architectural structure**—How will the site's pages be grouped to create themes and content silos? Some of these determinations might initially seem obvious, but the final decisions should take keyword research (covered in Truth 12, "Keywords are key") into account.

- **Create clean, valid code**—Search engines seem to prefer code that's lighter, cleaner, simpler, more semantically defined, and in accordance with World Wide Web Consortium (W3C) standards. The last thing you want is so much clunky code on the pages that it pushes all the keyword-rich content way down the page, where search engine crawlers won't be looking for it.

- **Use tables appropriately**—Tables distort the flow of HTML code and may push more important elements, such as body copy, further down the page than is desirable. Again, a CSS layout enables you to influence where in the code elements appear.

- **Avoid duplicate content**—Never have identical text content appear on multiple domains or within multiple pages on the same site. If there are various versions of your URL, choose one and redirect all the others to that URL or block the duplicates from the crawlers.

- **Follow proper site redirect architecture**—Avoid 302 (temporary) redirects. Instead, employ 301 (permanent) redirects to ensure that the search engines index the content appropriately.

- **Avoid Flash websites**—Flash sites often consist of only a single web page, even if the experience is rich enough to convey the feeling of a full site experience. There's no way a one-page website can rank for dozens of separate keywords.

- **Link internally**—In addition to a navigation menu, don't neglect opportunities to link internally to relevant areas of your website. Internal links are navigational shortcuts for visitors, and provide extra incentive for search engine crawlers to burrow deep into a site and find as many pages as possible.

- **Place nonessential graphics lower on the page**—Search engines index words, words, and more words. They pay the most attention to the words appearing at the top of each web page. So unless there's a compelling reason to use images on the northern end of a web page, place them a little further down.

- **Use individual title tags**—Every page on a site should have an individual and distinct title tag. (More on this in Truth 17, "What's in a title? Everything….")

- **Avoid dynamic URLs with multiple parameters, session IDs, and appended URLs**—URLs that constantly change rather than remain static throw obstacles into the paths of search engine crawlers, as well as tend to create duplicate content. If the navigation bar on a browser is full of nonsensical text, such as sid=LKJHLJUYIO483712345, it's time to reconsider that level of functionality.

- **Use strong templates**—Because templates affect the appearance, code, structure, and navigation of virtually every page on a site, the slightest change in a template can cause a radical change throughout the entire website. Create and code templates with the utmost care and attention to detail.

- **Use a flat file structure**—Ideally, URLs should be no more than three file levels deep and use hyphens rather than underscores to link keywords to the filenames.

- **Use breadcrumb navigation**—Keyword-rich breadcrumb navigation appears at the top of pages on many retail sites. It helps users understand where they are on a site, as well as providing a nice roadmap for crawlers. *Breadcrumbs* are hyperlinks rendered something like: Apparel: Women: Tops: Tshirts. The logic of the navigation is immediately apparent, and because each word is a link, it helps visitors and search engines alike find pages containing women's T-shirts.

TRUTH

11

Write for users and search engines will follow

High-quality, keyword-rich written content is the single most fundamental element of effective search engine optimization. Good copy is important to a website's users, too. Always bear in mind that search engines aren't actually using your website. People are. Websites must, therefore, be designed primarily with users in mind, but with heed paid to SEO tenets.

The same applies to website copy. Search engines don't read what's on a website—rather, they index the text. So although website copy should be written with users in mind first and search engines second, there are plenty of tips, tricks, and techniques that make persuasive, informative copy serve double duty and serve search engine optimization goals as well.

Always bear in mind that getting users to click that mouse to come to a website is only half the battle. Once there, they must be persuaded that they've come to the right place, as well as induced to take desired actions. Great copy pleases not only the search engines, but also a much more important constituency: the site's end users.

> Getting users to click that mouse to come to a website is only half the battle.

Website copy do's and don'ts

When writing copy for your site, use the following pointers to help you create copy that both speaks to your intended audience, as well as pays homage to the search engines:

- **Make copy keyword-rich**—Before picking up a pen (or firing up a computer), make sure you've thoroughly researched the keywords and phrases (discussed in Truth 12, "Keywords are key") that serves the website's goals, and that those key words match what its target audience is typing into search query boxes when they seek the information, products, or services that site offers.

- **Use keywords and phrases high on the page**—Search engine crawlers might spider a page all the way down to the very last word. Or they might not. So don't hold those keywords back. When crawlers visit a page, they pay attention to, as well as assign more value to, the words and phrases that "lead" the copy on a given page. Make an effort to kick off with the essentials. This isn't only good SEO advice; it will likely be helpful to visitors as well.

- **Use variations of keyword phrases**—Do not rely on the search engines' capability to stem words for you. Add your own plurals, tenses, and gerunds (words ending in "ing"). The difference between "hamster" and "hamsters" is subtle, but irregular plurals, such as "mouse" and "mice" or "goose" and "geese" differ radically as potential keywords. If a keyword has multiple potential spellings (for example, "web cam" and "webcam"), use both variations—just don't put both variations on the same page, because that appears sloppy and unprofessional to end users.

- **Use semantically related phrases**—Search engines use something called *latent semantic indexing (LSI)*, which helps determine a web page's rank by looking for related words in its content, or words in similar positions in other related documents. For example, if you have a page about a computer, semantically related words include computing, PC, computers, hardware, laptop, PC, PCs, computers, computings, hard drive, monitor, mouse, keypad, screen, Ethernet, USB, cable, disk, CD, CD_ROM, CD-ROM, and so on. LSI might lower the value of pages that match one specific term, but don't back it up with related terms.

- **Be descriptive**—Don't refer to "our team" when you can say "XYZ Corporation's search engine marketing experts." Why write "we" when you could use "Acme Bank of Akron, Ohio?" Now that you've done all that keyword research, use those terms wherever possible!

- **Use phrases instead of single keywords when possible**— Searchers often don't type single-word queries into search boxes, so use phrases whenever appropriate. "Small business loans" is more relevant to a searcher than "loans."

- **Never present text as a graphic**—It can't be repeated often enough: Search engines read text, not images. If the only instances of a company name appearing on a website is an image file of the corporate logo, as far as the search engines are concerned, that name isn't on the site at all. When using graphics, never, ever neglect properly naming and tagging the file (see Truth 19, "Tag images, audio, video, and other media").

- **Include a physical location**—"XYZ Corporation's San Francisco headquarters" works a lot better than "our office," particularly when you're trying to attract a local business clientele. You might also consider a footer containing a physical address, postal code, and phone number with area code.

- **Check your spelling**—When a search query is misspelled or mistyped, a "did you mean...?" message appears atop the search results page to help searchers refine their queries. Site owners, meanwhile, are on their own. Don't count on someone finding you via your mutual ability to misspell the same word in the same way. Get spelling and grammar right on the site.

- **Mind the snippets**—After the page title, a search engine snippet is your best shot at getting a searcher to click. A *snippet* is that short bit of descriptive text found in nearly every search engine result. One of the best ways to control your search engine snippet is with a unique description meta tag for every page.

- **Meta, title, and description tags**—Attention should be paid to crafting copy for meta, title, and description tags for each page. This will be discussed in depth in Truth 17, "What's in a title? Everything...," and Truth 18, "The relative importance of meta tags."

TRUTH

12

Keywords are key

Strong, optimized copy is the most critical part of any SEO initiative. But before the first sentence, tagline, or headline is written, you must first venture into the heart of search optimization by identifying those keywords and key phrases your target audience is likely to use when searching both for your website, and for individual pages within the site.

These are the words and phrases searchers use, not necessarily the ones you use back at the office when you're talking with your colleagues. Perhaps you're a medical professional who bandies about terms such as "myocardial infraction." The average Web searcher is more likely to seek information on "heart attack." While in the throes of home renovations, I once spent several weeks conducting search after search for "kitchen cabinet handles." It was only by accident that I learned the industry that manufactures and sells them refers to them as "pulls."

Who knew? I didn't. I just knew I wanted to buy them. In search, that's ultimately what counts.

Fredrick Marckini, who founded search engine marketing firm iProspect, tells the story of a meeting with a client, a lender, who wanted to be number one in search results for "loans." He had to explain to them that searchers are more inclined to "borrow" money.

The keywords and phrases that make a site visible to searchers aren't necessarily the terms you use. They're the terms that searchers use. Forget about the language used inside your company. Toss out the industry jargon. Instead, embark on a serious keyword research project.

> The keywords and phrases that make a site visible to searchers aren't the terms you use. They're the terms that searchers use.

The first step in this process is to simply brainstorm a list of the words and phrases a searcher might use to find your site or business. The trick here is to be specific. Forget broad terms, such as "shoes." Focus instead on "running shoes" or "wedding shoes" or "Nike running shoes" or "black patent leather high-heeled pumps." It can be helpful to ask outsiders such as friends, family, clients, or colleagues what terms come to mind.

Once the initial list is in hand, the next step is to determine how useful these terms really are. That's where keyword research tools come in handy. (A list of free and commercial tools is included in Appendix A, "Resources," located online at www.informit.com/title/9780789738318.) By running the list of proposed keywords through a keyword research tool, you'll learn how many searchers are actually conducting searches for that term every day, how many of those searches actually took action (for example, purchased the item), and other analytical information. These tools might also make you aware of words not on the list, or synonyms.

This information should narrow down the selections to the final list of keywords for the website. Plug these into a spreadsheet that helps you to visualize at a glance each word or phrase's search volume, competition, and conversion rate (if there is a history). This list will help narrow your focus and concentrate on the most important terms for your site. Don't completely eliminate very broad terms such as "shoes"—this helps searchers get a general feel for the site. But it's the very specific, targeted terms ("pink suede ballerina flats size 7") that attract the targeted traffic at the bottom of the purchase funnel.

The best keywords contain the following:

- Strong relevance to your site; terms for which you have content to support.
- Relatively high search volume; these are terms people actually search for.
- Relatively low competition; terms with a small number of search results.

Without careful research, you risk landing at the undesirable extremes of keywords. Either the terms will be so broad that you don't stand a chance of ranking for them in the search engines, and other sites are competing for them, or alternately, the terms are so specific that they're at the top of the search results—only no one's. searching for them.

Use the final list sparingly. Each page on the site should contain no more than 4–5 keywords. There should be relevant copy around each one, ideally high up on the page. Most search experts agree the keywords should appear in the first 100–200 words on the page.

In addition, use keywords in the following page elements:

- Title tag
- Description tags
- Meta keywords tag
- Headings
- Alt text
- Anchor text/navigational links

Done? Not so fast. Researching and optimizing keywords is a process that changes over time. As a website grows and develops, and products and customer needs change, so must a keyword list evolve over time. Some businesses create keyword calendars to reflect seasonal changes in their business cycle, bringing out Halloween-related keywords in the autumn, or cold- and flu-related terms in the winter months.

As with all aspect of online copy, use keywords wisely, and with a judicious amount of moderation. In SEO, the term *keyword density* refers to the percentage of times a keyword or phrase appears on a page compared to the total number of words in a page. If keywords appear too often, search engine spiders may assume you're practicing "keyword stuffing," and actually reduce that page's ranking for the relevant keyword(s). Of course, this can only happen when imprudent—or unethical—websites optimize for search engines at the expense of the user. Optimal keyword density is highly debated. Generally speaking, 5 to 8 percent keyword density in body copy is considered good without going overboard. A number of free tools to check keyword density are listed in Appendix A located online at www.informit.com/title/9780789738318. Many of these take the keywords placed in tags and hyperlinks into consideration, as well as the visible text on each page of a site.

TRUTH
13

Use analytics and keyword research tools

Brainstorming exercises, together with surveying family, friends, clients, and co-workers, is a great place to start researching the right keywords for your website. Another integral part of this process is using the right tools.

One of the best places to start is with whatever third-party web analytics application you're currently using to measure and monitor your site. (You are using an analytics solution, aren't you?) Every commercial analytics package on the market, as well as free solutions such as Google Analytics, capture the actual keywords searchers used in search engines to find pages on your site and actually clicked. Usually, this information will be broken down between organic searches and clicks from paid search advertising campaigns, should you be running those.

Of course, analytics will only tell how the site is reacting to search engines now. They do not address its potential. A poorly optimized site displays very few keywords in the log files. Still, it's a start.

The larger and more diverse the website, the longer the list of organic keywords will tend to be. Smaller, more specialized sites will have shorter lists. Either way, learning which keywords drive a site's organic search traffic not only reveals a great deal about how searchers are finding the site, but also about how the site is showing up in organic search listings. The process will also reveal which pages are getting the most organic traffic, as well as which pages aren't. This, in turn, might influence how individual pages are optimized.

> The process will also reveal which pages are getting the most organic traffic, as well as which pages aren't.

Another metric that shouldn't be overlooked by SEO professionals in a site's log files is the time users spent on individual pages. This is particularly true if they arrived on a page directly from a search engine. Of course, the time-spent metric can have other implications in addition to those discussed here. When searchers arrive on a page, are they spending an acceptable amount of time there, perhaps proceeding deeper into the site, or do they bail out almost immediately? The amount of time a searcher should spend on a page varies greatly, of course. Common sense dictates that a publisher would want a visitor to invest time in, say, reading an article, while a "Contact Us" page might require much less of an investment of a visitor's time.

Overall, a properly optimized page will ensure that a visitor spends an appropriate amount of time on it, or follows the links on the page. That metric indicates their needs

> Overall, a properly optimized page will ensure that a visitor spends an appropriate amount of time on it, or follows the links on the page.

are being satisfied because the page they arrived at is relevant to the expectations that were raised by the organic search listing.

The other primary destination for keyword research are the tools specifically designed for the purpose. An extensive list of these appears in Appendix A, "Resources," (located online at www.informit.com/title/9780789738318) but let's take a look at some of the most popular (and powerful) free, web-based keyword research tools:

- **Google's Keyword Tool** is primarily intended to help Google's paid search advertisers, but anyone optimizing a site for organic search should give it a whirl. Enter a term such as "life insurance," and you get a list back of hundreds of related keyword phrases (life insurance, term life insurance, life insurance quote, and life insurance quotes are the top five at press time). Together with this information, Google displays the advertiser competition (the relative number of advertisers bidding for the term) and the relative search volumes for both the past month and year.

- **Wordtracker's** free tool (a more robust commercial application is also available) collects search terms on a weekly basis from the major metacrawlers—Dogpile and Metacrawler. That same lookup reveals exactly how many searches were conducted on life insurance, term life insurance, whole life insurance, life insurance companies, and life insurance quotes over the past seven days across these search engines.

- **Trellian's Keyword Discovery Free Search Term Suggestion Tool** collects data from dozens of search engines worldwide and tells you the annual number of searches for the top terms generated from its data: life insurance, life insurance settlement, term life insurance, whole life insurance, and life insurance quotes. Only the top-five results of each keyword query are displayed here. Further down the lists returned by these different tools are results that vary more widely for a variety of reasons. For instance, Google's data is specific to its own search engine, whereas Wordtracker and Trellian collect search data from a broad variety of search sources. Search behavior is influenced by other factors, such as seasonality. You can bet terms such as "halloween costume" peak in the fall, and plummet in November, for example. And certainly those terms that are on the top of the list are far from the only ones for which a site might want to optimize. Optimization is not just a matter of going broad, if the goal is highly relevant, targeted traffic. Therefore, optimizing for "no exam life insurance" might not only be much easier, but also considerably more profitable, if that's what the site in question is selling, promoting, or providing content about.

> Only the top-five results of each keyword query are displayed here. Further down the lists returned by these different tools are results that vary more widely for a variety of reasons.

TRUTH

14

Site stats share the bad news, too

Just as analytics tools and site stats are an essential aid in optimizing a site's searchability, so too can these tools flag warning signs, bad news, and other signals that the website in question is not meeting searchers' expectations.

In such cases, bad news is not necessarily a bad thing. After all, we're talking search engine *optimization*. By definition, SEO is a continuous, ongoing process. Without any negatives, what would you optimize?

In the broadest sense, the goal of SEO is to increase organic search engine referrals to a given website. Therefore, tracking unique visitors from search engine referrals as a percentage of a site's total unique visitors is an essential part of measuring the success of any SEO effort. You want unique search engine referrals to rise, or at the very least to hold steady. It's worthwhile noting that unique search engine referrals are measured not in their totality but as a percentage of traffic because nearly every business is affected by cyclical variance, ranging from news cycles to seasonality. If the only thing you're selling is snow tires, you'd expect a decrease in traffic (as well as in snow tire-related searches) in the summer months, wouldn't you?

> By definition, SEO is a continuous, ongoing process. Without the negatives, what would you optimize?

The traffic to your site is rising steadily. Great news, right? Well, not so fast. If traffic to the website is going up, but sales, lead-generation, or the other goals of the website are flat or in decline, something's wrong. It could be site issues, of course, but if flat performance is directly linked to organic search engine referrals, it's all but a sure sign that the site has been optimized for the wrong keywords.

Keeping an eye on those pages users visit—and those they don't— is another important set of stats to track. Search engines drive traffic to specific pages in a site, not just to the homepage (see Truth 8, "You don't have a homepage anymore"). This holds advantages both for the user and for the site owner. Through search, users are able to navigate directly to the page that most specifically addresses their search query. They needn't bother to poke around a site to navigate to relevant information.

The edge for site owners is that each and every page of a website affords new and specific opportunities for optimization. Each page has a specific and individual set of keywords that can be adjusted and optimized. Copy can be revised and rewritten. Both outbound and inbound links can be improved. Certainly no site gets consistent levels of traffic across all pages. Some are simply bound to perform better than others. But that doesn't mean underperforming pages deserve to be ignored. They should be considered optimization opportunities.

Even the most rudimentary site analytics tools provide more data than many site owners are prepared to deal with. What matters is determining which datasets are important, and then carefully monitoring and tracking those statistics on a regular basis—daily is great; monthly at a bare minimum.

Overall, the most fundamental site elements to track include the following:

- **Visitors**—What could be more basic than knowing how many visitors have come to your site in a given time frame? Be careful to differentiate between unique (or individual visitors) and overall site visits, which account for the total number of visits to the site, combining unique visitors with people who visit multiple times. Although knowing the number of visitors to a site won't help increase conversions, it's a good indicator of how search engine rankings and links from other sites affect traffic.

- **Referrers**—Where's your site traffic coming from? This metric lets you know which search engines send how much traffic to your site, as well as which links to you on other sites impel users to visit.

- **Keywords**—Ranking well for keywords is one thing. Getting traffic from them can be something else altogether. Keyword stats— those words and phrases searchers are using to find you—let you know exactly how much traffic keyword rankings actually generate.

- **Time spent and bounce rates**—Traffic is only part of the goal. Encouraging visitors to actually stick around and do something, such as buying or otherwise converting, is a much more critical benchmark of site performance. Assessing how much time visitors spend on a given page, or on the site overall, is a strong indicator of how well it fulfills the expectations of users who followed a link from a search engine, or any other referrer, for that matter.

■ **Exit pages**—Exit pages can be a strong indicator of flaws in a website. This stat indicates pages, processes, or other flaws in a site that frustrate, annoy, confound, or disappoint visitors—enough so that they leave. A site page that does not indicate the end of a desired process (for example, the "Thank You" page that following a completed transaction) is likely not a good place to lose visitors. This metric is highly effective at revealing fundamental problem pages on a site.

After collecting the preceding data over several weeks, patterns should begin to emerge that should inform both the search optimization and site strategy. Here's a hypothetical example. Say a site was optimized for the phrases "video production services Cleveland" and "video post-production Cleveland." The site ranks well for both keyword phrases, and both generate a healthy amount of traffic. Yet while the first page generates leads (phone calls or filling out a form leading to a "Thank You" page on the site), the second phrase generates traffic, but no conversions.

You've got a problem. It could be a site issue, or perhaps a subtle optimization tweak is in order. Seasoned SEOs will tell you that even an apparently meaningless change, such as "video post-production services Cleveland" or "*digital* post-production Cleveland" or "video production Ohio," can do the trick.

The number of tweaks, adjustments, and calibrations you can make to any search optimization initiative approach the infinite. But without consistently tracking results with a web metrics program, it's simply impossible to know what works. And what doesn't.

TRUTH

15

Think twice about hot new technologies

Search engine spiders like big, dumb, ugly sites, remember? They like text, and they like links they can follow to discover new pages and other websites. Search engine crawlers care not a whit for lush photography and fancy-pants design elements.

But site owners, and often users, like glitz, glamour, and flash. And Flash, too, as this certainly applies to sites built in Macromedia Flash, which affords the opportunity to construct dazzling animations—for people, at least. Unfortunately, sites that rely too heavily on Flash can be all but invisible to the search engines.

> Search engine crawlers care not a whit for lush photography and fancy-pants design elements.

Flash

What does a search engine "see" when it encounters a Flash website? To find out, visit Nike.com. As the sites's Flash intro loads, take a look at the "page source" option in your browser. Here's a snippet of the not-so-flashy result:

```
<title>Nike.com</title>
        <meta http-equiv="Content-Type"
content="text/html; charset=UTF-8" />

        <script type="text/javascript" src="/
renov/common/js/utils.js"></script>
        <style type="text/css">
```

What a search engine spider "sees" is what it delivers. In Nike's case, it sees code—not text.

The site's organic listing description—remember, these descriptors are lifted from the page—doesn't fare much better. This is what appears in Google's search results:

```
Nike
failure; org.xml.sax.SAXParseException:
The reference to entity "re" must end with
the ';' delimite'r.
```

Nike, a huge global brand, can get away with this. Most businesses can't. It should also be noted that the major search engines can at least partially index sites built in Flash, but the operative word here is partially. If SEO is a *priority*, it's advisable not to build the site in Flash, or at the very least to embed Flash movies into pages on a plain, vanilla, text-rich HTML site rather than going whole Flash hog. Or if a site is to be built entirely in Flash, be sure to build individual site pages rather than create a site that's one big movie (ergo, one big page), even if transitions make it appear to viewers that multiple pages are going by. Or consider building an alternative non-Flash site, which can be done relatively easily.

This strategy helps redeem Nike.com. Under the nonsensical site descriptor, the following helpful navigation to section pages within the nike.com domain appears:

```
Nike's Official Online Store
Women
NikeStore
Nikeid


Hear How You Run
Running
Nikefootball
Soccer
More results from nike.com »
```

Although these sections are built in Flash as well, as least the search engines know they're there from searchers clicking through to these pages.

Some experts advocate building two versions of the same site: one in Flash, and the other in HTML. Visitors can select their preference on the homepage, which should be keyword rich and contain a link to a site map to allow search engine spiders to burrow down into all the HTML pages. If adopting this strategy, it's imperative to submit only the HTML site to the search engines to index.

With Flash, the same URL can deliver varying content. This presents obstacles to crawlers, as well as to optimization. The same problems hold true with other rich web technologies and applications such as AJAX and Silverlight.

AJAX

AJAX (an acronym for Asynchronous JavaScript and XML) applications have exploded in popularity in recent years, thanks to their capability to provide smooth and seamless browsing experiences. A prime example of an AJAX Web experience is Google maps. You can zoom in and out or right and left smoothly, rather than the clicking, waiting, and then clicking some more sequence of "traditional" web browsing.

Silverlight

Microsoft's Silverlight is a cross-browser, cross-platform, cross-device plug-in that delivers eye-popping media experiences and rich online interactive applications. It's growing in popularity with advertisers but should be approached with the same degree of caution by those whose priority is a well-optimized, search-friendly website.

As with Flash, a better approach to AJAX and Silverlight is to embed these interesting and very often useful tools into big, dumb, ugly, but beautiful to search engines (and users, too) HTML websites.

TRUTH

16

Content management systems matter—a lot

Let's say you want to bake a cake. Before you do, you need to buy a cake ring. You conduct a quick search on the Web and find two different merchants at two different domains offering just what you need. Here are the URLs of the two product pages you found:

http://www.domain.com/store/cake-rings.html
http://www.domain.com/detail.asp?id=114&trng=fgle

Later, your daughter needs some help with her homework assignment on global warming, so you help her to search current news stories about the issue. You find two very useful articles from two separate publications at these URLs:

http://domain.com/news/thegreatbeyond/ 2008/04/ update_storm_over_globalwarming.html

http://www.domain.com/disp/story.mpl/front/ 5736103.html

In both the preceding cases, the URLs were automatically generated by the website owner's content management system (CMS).

Both in e-commerce and in publishing, there's a world of difference between search-friendly URLs (which, by the way, just so happen to be user-friendly as well) and a gobbledygook alphabet soup that will click through to the right page, but has none of the benefits that a simplified URL structure confers to search engine spiders and actual human beings alike.

Generating URLs is only part of the functionality of a CMS. Effectively, a CMS houses the structure and templates of a website, thus enabling a user, or group of users, to input content with relatively little skill, coding ability, or technical knowledge.

> ...there's a world of difference between search-friendly URLs and gobbledygook alphabet soup that will click through to the right page.

A properly chosen and configured CMS can address both site-wide and individual page issues that affect search engines' capability to effectively find, crawl, and index a website. Although SEO considerations are one of many factors that go into the selection and configuration of a CMS, it's important to bear them in mind if SEO is a priority.

In addition to generating search engine-friendly static URLs, other site-wide SEO considerations in selecting and configuring a CMS include the following:

- **Managing dynamic URLs**—Although static URLS are preferable from the standpoint of search engines, for some sites, dynamic URLs are inevitable. This is particularly true for internal site pages that are generated on-the-fly as the result of a site search (for example, "plaid winter coat"). CMS systems can be configured to generate friendlier-looking alias URLs for these dynamic pages.

- **Site map**—This is used to help crawlers find all content on the website, accessible via a single link. Most CMS systems can automatically generate a site map.

- **Text navigation**—This ensures that the main site navigation is rendered in text rather than graphically to aid crawlers.

- **Flat navigation**—Constructing directories no more than two or three levels deep can help search engines to assign more import to pages that aren't "buried" in the site. An example of this might be domain.com/televisions/Sony/ModelNumber as opposed to: domain.com/televisions/color/flatscreen/plasma/32"/Sony/ModelNumber

- **Manage broken links**—Broken or outdated internal links are a road to nowhere for crawlers, and can lead to reduced search engine rankings site-wide. Links must convey relevance, not dead ends. Therefore, a CMS should have a process in place for finding and eliminating broken links, as well as custom 404 (error) pages.

On-page optimization factors in a CMS include the following:

- **Meaningful title tags**—If you're publishing an article about global warming, "update_storm_over_globalwarming" is a fantastic title tag for the page, for both the user and the search engine crawler. For reasons that by now should be patently obvious, "story.mpl/front/5736103.html" is anything but a desirable page title. The text in a title tag is one of the single most important factors in ranking; thus, this function should be deemed mission critical.

- **Effective meta tags and descriptors**—Meta tags and descriptors (see Truth 18, "The relative importance of meta tags") provide search engines with the descriptive data that describes a page's content in search engine results, as well as supply other descriptive keywords and phrases. Some CMS systems are configured to generate this information automatically; others enable users to create and input the descriptors. Either way, meta data is a highly important component of any CMS.

- **Alt attributes**—Search engine crawlers can't read graphics, photos, movies, or audio files, but they can understand the "alt attributes" associated with such content. A CMS should ensure that nontext elements are properly labeled.

- **Clean and lean code**—Cascading style sheets (CSS) and JavaScript templates eliminate the need for top-heavy coding on pages, making meaty, relevant content information and links easier for crawlers to find and index.

- **Spell check**—Spelling errors aren't just unprofessional and sloppy looking to human users, but they're confusing to search engines, too.

All content management systems aren't created equal, particularly when it comes to search engine optimization.

All content management systems aren't created equal, particularly when it comes to search engine optimization—and price isn't a determinant. Some of the costliest commercial CMS packages are all but useless when it comes to SEO, whereas some of the search-friendliest CMSs are absolutely free blog platforms.

Does SEO matter to you? If so, then choose your CMS wisely.

TRUTH

17

What's in a title?
Everything...

Ask a group of search engine optimization specialists what the one single most important factor is in determining high rankings—or at the very least, search results page relevance—and you are likely to get a consistent answer. Chances are, most will vote for the modest—but mighty—title tag.

The text in each page's title tag is what appears in the clickable link on search engine results pages. So, fixing and adjusting the words that are used (and appear) in a page's title tag is one of the quickest and most effective adjustments you can make to influence not only that page's ranking, but also the number of people who actually click on the link. Just as important, title tags, both individually and in aggregate, help search engines and searchers alike to understand what the website is about.

A title tag is a basic element of every online HTML page. In HTML code, a title tag is the first text in the page header. It looks like this:

```
<head>
<title> Here's Where the Title Goes </title>
</head>
```

So what goes into a title tag, anyway?

It's hard to think of an example in which the name of the company, organization, or even the individual behind the website in question shouldn't be at least a component of the title tag. A title should be inserted for every title tag on every page of the site, particularly if the site is commercial in nature. And as mentioned earlier, search engines place more weight on the words and phrases that appear on the top of a page than they do to the words further down. Therefore, most SEO specialists recommend that the brand or company name be the very first word or part of the first phrase in every title tag.

In terms of actual characters in the title tag, you don't have a whole lot of leeway. Most experts recommend limiting title tag text to about 65 characters (including spaces). Otherwise, you risk your title ending with "...." The various search engines occasionally adjust how many characters they allow to appear in title tags, but browser windows are just so wide. Limit text to 8–10 words, and you should be fine. And after a page is indexed, you can always check to see if the entire title tag actually appears as a clickable link.

Others argue that if the brand or company name is part of the site's domain, the most important keywords or phrases should hold precedence.

Hopefully, your title tags are considerably less than the 65-character maximum.

Don't limit your tags to the company name. Each page of a site provides a new opportunity for an individualized, highly relevant, keyword-rich title tag. By no means should you let that opportunity slip.

How would this work in practice? For example, the law firm, Stevens, Brown, and Partners, a law firm in Seattle specializing in litigation, might use any of the following variants for the title tags:

- Stevens, Brown, and Partners - Seattle lawyers - Law Firm

- Stevens, Brown, and Partners - Seattle lawyer - Jon Stevens bio

- Stevens, Brown, and Partners | litigation attorneys | Seattle, WA

- Stevens, Brown, and Partners - Washington state litigation

- Stevens, Brown, and Partners, Seattle legal representation

- Stevens, Brown, and Partners; Seattle WA lawsuit

- Stevens, Brown, and Partners › Contact a Seattle Attorney

- Stevens, Brown, and Partners/ WA Personal Injury Lawyers

Note the use of separators, including hyphens, commas, colons, semicolons, arrows, and dividing lines in the text. These separators count toward the character allowance; however, they also help a searcher to quickly scan and comprehend the search result. The actual keywords that appear in the title tag will be heavily influenced

> Actual keywords that appear in the title tag will be heavily influenced not only by the content on individual pages, but also by the keyword research.

not only by the content on individual pages, but also by the keyword research that's gone into crafting the copy on site pages, as well as the target audience.

Are people searching for lawyer or lawyers, attorney or attorneys, law firm, or a combination of all these words? Keyword research reveals this information and, of course, helps to inform title tag construction.

Generic information such as "about" or "homepage" or "contact" reveals very little to searchers or to search engines about a page's content or context. Just 5 to 10 seconds of thought is usually enough to help you come up with the right title tag. "About the law firm" or "How to contact a Seattle attorney" are both much more descriptive, relevant, and helpful phrases.

Our hypothetical law firm might be trying to attract clients in the Seattle metro area, or across Washington state (but not in Washington, DC, which is a very important distinction). These priorities and criteria help to shape title tag strategy and content.

And sometimes, if a long keyword phrase is particularly effective and relevant, it might be a good idea to chuck a brand or company name to get the longer title in, something along the lines of "Find an attorney for a personal injury lawsuit in Seattle, WA."

Don't get bent out of shape over title tags. There's probably no absolutely perfect page title.

All this being said, don't get bent out of shape over title tags. There's probably no absolutely perfect page title. Some might rank higher, whereas others might get more clicks. It's a trade-off. You can always test and tweak title tag variations.

In title tags, as well as in keywords anywhere on a site, don't forget that stop words don't count toward SEO.

What's a stop word? It's one of the 500 or so most common words in the English language—so common, in fact, search engines simply ignore them. This includes words like the, and, is, from, to, always, never, and so on. Absolutely use these when necessary for end users, of course, but bear in mind that search engines are programmed to ignore them more or less entirely.

Never forget that title tags are just that: titles. It's, therefore, probably not a good idea to title a site page before it's already been written and optimized. The information on each individual page is one of the most important determining factors of what should go into the title of that page. If there's so much information that you can't determine what the title ought to be, it's probably wise to rewrite the copy, or even to create two or more separate pages on the site, so both the copy and the title tags can be better optimized and positioned.

The relative importance of meta tags

Long, long ago, back in the mid-1990s, when search was young and the Internet bubble hadn't burst, meta data was an important factor in search engine rankings. Although that's no longer the case, ignoring meta tags in an SEO endeavor is not a good idea either. To find out why, let's look at what meta tags are, and learn a little bit about their history, as well as their use in the here and now.

In the early days of the Web, HTML meta tags began to be incorporated into web page header information. Meta tags were and are included right along with the title tag, which was discussed in the previous Truth. However, it is important to note that title tags and meta tags are not one and the same. The function of meta tags is to help webmasters, as well as search engines, understand more about the web page. The text in meta tags is not displayed on the actual web page but is easily revealed by viewing the "page source" option in any web browser.

There are quite a few different elements of meta data, and not all of them are relevant to search. For instance, the meta language tag, a two-letter abbreviation that specifies the primary language the page copy is in, isn't always relevant to search unless the site is multilingual. Or the meta revisit-after tag, which instructs search engines to recrawl the page's content after a specified period of time (for example, a day, week, or month). The only problem with the meta revisit tag? It isn't supported by any search engine. Moreover, it never was supported, and most probably never will be supported by a search engine.

Clearly, there's no use discussing all the types of meta tags out there. For search engine optimization, only three meta tags are worth discussing—and only two of them really matter. Still, there are so many misconceptions about meta tags out there, it's worthwhile discussing how all three can, and can't, influence search engine optimization.

Meta robots tag

This tag is used only if you do not want pages indexed by search engines (and this is often the case). How and when to use this tag is discussed in Truth 51, "Sometimes you don't want to be found."

Meta keywords tag

This tag contains the major keywords and key phrases on which a
webmaster, publisher, or SEO wants a page to be found when they're
used in a search query, as well as rank highly in organic search
results. For certain keywords, you just stick them in this meta tag and
you're golden, right?

Not so fast. If it sounds too good to be true, it probably is. In
the case of meta keyword tags, this is one of the biggest SEO
misconceptions. Years ago, people started to abuse meta keyword
tags by filling them with useless or irrelevant words to achieve
a higher rank. This worked...for a very short while. Thanks to the
abusers, most major search engines (Google in particular) place little
to no importance on the meta keywords tag. The best advice: Don't
bother. It's no longer worth it.

Meta description tag

This is the tag that matters most, and it's well worth taking the
time to craft a good page description. That's because the text that
comprises the description is displayed in search results just under
the clickable title. Here's an example—in this case, the first result on
Yahoo! from a real Seattle-based personal injury lawyer's website.
The original query was for "seattle personal injury lawyer." If you
conduct this search yourself, note how Yahoo! highlights these terms
in the text to indicate relevance with the search query:

```
Seattle Personal Injury
Hire an experienced personal injury lawyer for
all your legal needs. Bradley Johnson Attorneys
provides personal injury representation in
Western Washington. Call today.
www.personalinjurylawwashington.com
```

On the same day, Google delivered a different number-one result, but
the meta description tag data appears in the description and also
highlights the matching keywords in the query:

```
Seattle Personal Injury Lawyer | Seattle
Washington Personal...
Contact a Seattle accident attorney
experienced in many aspects of personal
injury law including, but not limited to,
premises liability, car and truck...
seattle.injuryboard.com
```

It's important to think of the meta description tag as a brief advertisement or call-to-action.

Although the meta description tag is not always featured on the search results page, it happens reliably enough to make this page element critical in SEO. The meta description tag may not be as much an influencer in actual results ranking as other elements such as title tags, page copy, and links, but because it's the information a searcher sees about a search result (together with the page title), it's a tremendous influencer when it comes to whether that user will click.

It's, therefore, important to think of the meta description tag as a brief advertisement or call-to-action where the searcher is concerned. So, although it's critical that the descriptive copy be honest, it can also be important to get a bit sexy—or persuasive (without going overboard, of course)—to drive traffic. Bear in mind as well that the meta description remains just that: a description. It's not, nor is it intended to be, an actual ad. If the description misleads people or misrepresents a page's content, they're only one click away from leaving. Stay honest and straightforward.

Equally important when writing descriptions is to use keywords. As we've seen previously, matched search keywords are bolded. These can be quite persuasive when it comes to driving traffic from search results pages.

And as with titles, the goal is to accomplish these ends in very limited space. At present, Google displays up to 160 characters of a meta description tag (including spaces). Yahoo! shows up to 165 characters, whereas MSN will display more than 200. Google is the yardstick here. Stick to 160 characters or less.

And don't forget that as with titles, every site page that you want users to find—and to click on—in search engines warrants its own carefully crafted and considered meta description.

Although it's critical that the descriptive copy be honest, it can also be important to get a bit sexy...or persuasive.

TRUTH

19

Tag images, audio, video, and other media

If you've read any of the other truths in this book, you've probably seen one particular truism mentioned more than any other: the fact that search engines can't "read" anything but plain old text.

A website can teem with lush images, arresting graphics, eye-catching video, toe-tapping music, or fascinating audio interviews and discourses. A page can offer downloads of media, including documents, presentations, spreadsheets, and what-have-you, but as far as search engines are concerned, these are all just so many random bits and bytes. A fundamental component of any SEO strategy is to work to make these diverse types of files count toward search visibility.

Making files accessible

First and foremost, ensure that the file or directory in which media files are stored on your server is open and accessible to search engines, and not blocked by a robots.txt file (see Truth 51, "Sometimes you don't want to be found"). Also, if you use thumbnail images, don't put the "click to enlarge image" link inside a JavaScript link (a common mistake). When this occurs, search engines cannot access the larger file.

Naming media files

After ensuring that search engines can actually get to media files, plain old text—the fundamental building block of search—is naturally the best place to start optimizing the files themselves. What all these file types have in common is a need for clear, descriptive names or titles. In no case should you use the default name spit out by audio, video, or image software, such as img230769.jpg. The names of these types of files should be as descriptive as possible and match what the file represents.

If you have an image of an apple, for example, call it a "New York State Granny Smith Apple," or "Olsen Orchard's Ripe Macintosh Apple," not just plain old "apple." For all a search engine knows, this "apple" could be a computer. Or even the Beatles' record label.

Such descriptive names are not only found by search engine spiders, but often have the added advantage of appearing above, below, or near the image itself, enhancing the user experience as well. Filenames are accorded a lot of weight by search engines when it comes to ranking.

It should, therefore, come as no surprise that those websites that regularly use multiple media files require a naming strategy or protocol to ensure consistency in the names used for graphics, audio, or video.

Adding meta data

After giving media files clear, descriptive names, don't forget to add more descriptive text (or meta data) to the "alt" attribute in the file's tag. Make it short and to the point, such as with the filename. This is an opportunity to go a little bit broader. That Granny Smith apple, for example, might be from Olsen's Orchards, or have been a product of the 2008 harvest, or perhaps this is the place to indicate that it's a sweet, crisp, delicious, and nutritious apple. Online merchants might want to use this field to add information such as a manufacturer, product category, or UPC code. Let's say you sell DVDs online. The name of the media file—in this case, a photo of the cover art—would obviously be the title of the film. The "alt" attribute might include the names of the actors, director, studio, genre, release year, and any miscellaneous information such as "Academy Award Nominee."

Perhaps the media file in question is an interview with Tom Cruise by Oprah Winfrey, and the file is named "Interview with Tom Cruise." The meta data might refer to the film or topic the actor discusses in the interview, refer to the name of the interviewer (boom—you're found in searches for "Oprah Winfrey"), or list some of the actor's credits so that the video shows up on more general searches by the actor's fans.

Keyword strategy, combined with the site's goals, will help you decide what type of additional data are added in this section.

Adjacent captions

A caption adjacent to the media file also helps search engines to

> Don't forget to add more descriptive text (or meta data) to the "alt" attribute in the file's tag.

> The goal here is to function much like a newspaper or a magazine by adding keyword-rich captions to media files.

"understand" what the file is about, because adjacent text helps search engines contextualize what they've found and determine relevancy. The goal here is to function much like a newspaper or a magazine by adding keyword-rich captions to media files. By adding adjacent text, even if you've been careless and named an image file "Bass.jpg," adjacent text and captions can help a search engine understand if the image depicts a fish, a musical instrument, or even a particular brand of shoe. This approach can be broadened to optimize the entire page the media file resides on in a website to further increase the depth of context and relevancy.

Choosing the right file type

In the case of images, file type matters. Photos should be rendered in JPG format, and logos should be GIF files. The reason is simply that these are standard formats that search engines "expect." Search engines assume that a GIF file has 256 colors, standard for rendering graphics such as logos, while photos are rendered in millions of colors. And when using logo files, it's all-important that the file be named with whatever's in that logo. No search engine is smart enough to deduce that a simple GIF file represents the logo for Ford, or Sony, or Acme Exterminating.

Posting transcripts

Although it can be labor-intensive, posting an HTML transcript of the dialogue in an audio or video file goes extraordinarily far in terms of optimizing the actual content of these media files. Given the nature of the medium, it's best to keep these files short, optimally five minutes or less (particularly in the case of video). Cutting longer media files into shorter segments not only eases viewing, but also affords additional opportunities to optimize the content and to provide extra, spider-able links between episodes or installments. This is particularly helpful in the case of episodic videos or sites that offer podcasts.

TRUTH

Some links are more equal than others

A solid link strategy is essential to SEO. Links— inbound, outbound, and internal—lie at the heart of any SEO effort. No well-optimized website or page is an island. As discussed earlier, links are the information roads and streets of the information superhighway, so to speak. Only by following links to pages from other links are search engine spiders able to navigate the vast cosmos of the Internet and find all that content that they index.

Spiders also use these links to weed out obsolete content from its index. That's why linking from existing sites to a brand-new website can help it get indexed very quickly. There are no guarantees, of course, but I've seen sites appear in Google's index in two to three days after they were linked to.

This is, in fact, in keeping with Google's own recommendations to webmasters, as follows:

> Only by following links to pages from other links are search engine spiders able to navigate the vast cosmos of the Internet....

> "The best way to ensure Google finds your site is for your page to be linked from lots of pages on other sites. Google's robots jump from page to page on the web via hyperlinks, so the more sites that link to you, the more likely it is that we'll find you quickly."

Links are also an essential factor that search engine algorithms use to determine the ranking of a website or page. Should it be result #1, or appear buried on page 22 of the search results for a given query?

Inbound links to your site—that is, other web pages and sites that link to yours—are something search engines deem akin to votes. Others use the analogy of a popularity contest. Links say, "Hey! Click over to this page. It matters. It contains information you might be interested in taking a look at. If you think our page here is worthwhile, we recommend that you take a look at that page over there."

Search engines determine ranking in part based on the number of links pointing to your site. But simply having inbound links to your site isn't enough. In the world of search, it's not just quantity—it's the quality of links that matter. This is where a link strategy gets, well, strategic.

Not all links are created equal.

> In the world of search, it's not just quantity—it's the quality of links that matter.

There are lots and lots of different types of links, of course. There are also links that have no influence whatsoever in SEO that you still wouldn't say no to. A link in an e-mail newsletter, for example, can generate lots of quality traffic without Yahoo!, Microsoft, or Google having the slightest idea it exists.

Search engines weigh links to your site from other websites based on the quality of the inbound link. So, what's a quality link? Only the search engine companies themselves know for sure how their algorithms (which are secret) work. However, sites with high PageRank (see Truth 39, "Don't live and die by PageRank") are likely to confer the highest-quality links. In the broadest possible terms, a quality link comes from a prestigious, authoritative website that contains content that's contextually relevant to the content on your own site. If your site examines news or current affairs, a link from *The New York Times* or *The Wall Street Journal* is of infinitely higher value than a link from a site that sells cleaning supplies, or one from a scarcely read, seldom-updated blog. In advertising parlance, every link could be considered to be an endorsement. The best links are something akin to celebrity endorsements.

> In advertising parlance, every link could be considered to be an endorsement. The best links are something akin to celebrity endorsements.

Of course, not every site is going to get a *NYT* or *WSJ* link, nor do they need to. What the search engines are looking for is something akin to a popularity contest. Links are reputation enhancing, and help search engines determine how important a page is. Are the links to your sites relevant? Do they come from sites that have relevant or related content? What's in the text that actually surrounds the link? It matters. Think back to that site selling cleaning supplies. It may be the most popular supplier of brooms and mops on the Web, but a link from a page about brooms and mops to a page on your site discussing foreign economic relations is not going to do much for your ranking.

On the other hand, links between our broom and mop purveyor and a website offering cleaning services are more than appropriate. Ditto for links in this constellation from "how to get stuff clean" pages. These sites could include dealers in other types of housewares, sites that talk about getting the right tools for a specific cleaning job, sites that sell detergents and soaps, or news stories about the company selling those mops and brooms.

All these kinds of sites (and likely more) are in the relevant linking realm. All would serve to boost the mops and brooms site's visibility and relevancy with search engines.

A very basic approach to getting relevant sites to link to you is to appropriately link to them. Searching for your target keywords on the major search engines will quickly reveal the most relevant sites and pages. The higher they rank in the search results, the more relevant the search engines consider them to be. Visit and assess these pages, and drop a personalized note to the site owner to politely request a link. If you've linked to them, show them where by providing the URL (more on reciprocal linking in Truth 24, "Share and share alike: Reciprocal linking").

Another good place to start is a quick check of who's already linking to you. A number of link analysis tools can perform this function, or you can simply search Google or Yahoo! using this link: www.YourDomain.com.

TRUTH

21

Building links through online directories

If inbound links are one of the fastest ways to inclusion in search engine indices, online directory listings are one of the fastest means to that end.

Of course, just as all links aren't created equal, neither are all online directories—of which there are thousands. You could, of course, submit your site to every directory out there. But going under the assumption that your time and resources are in shorter supply than the sheer number of directories on the Internet, it would be wise to take a more considered approach.

A logical place to start is by submitting to the Open Directory Project (www.dmoz.org), which calls itself "the largest, most comprehensive human-edited directory of the Web." Its data powers the core directory services for many of the Web's major search engines, including Google, AOL Search, Netscape Search, and Alexa.

The Open Directory Project is the only major online directory that's free, which is both good news and bad. Often called DMOZ or referred to as ODP, it's constructed and maintained by a vast community of volunteer human editors. (We can put those scurrying spiders to rest in this section!) So, although no money changes hands in exchange for a listing, the lapse between submission and inclusion can range from a few days to—brace yourself—even years.

That's why very often, the first stop on the SEO directory odyssey is Yahoo!. Its size and scope rival DMOZ, and like the Open Directory, the Yahoo! Directory is human-edited. It's possible to submit a site for free, but many commercial sites find it worthwhile to fast-track their listing by paying a nonrefundable $299 fee. This ensures that the site will be reviewed for inclusion (provided it doesn't feature adult content or services), but it does not

…the lapse between submission and inclusion [in DMOZ] can range from a few days to—brace yourself—even years.

guarantee that the site will actually be included in the directory. If it is included, the listing can be edited, recategorized, or removed at any time at the discretion of the editors.

So why would anyone pay Yahoo! $299 for what could amount to...nothing? Assuming the submitted site is legitimate, it most likely will be included. And once it's in Yahoo!'s directory, the listing will be indexed by Google as well.

Other general directories you might consider include Starting Point, ExactSeek, and Best of the Web.

Although listings in general directories such as DMOZ and Yahoo! are valuable, high-quality and well-trafficked directories that are relevant to a website's content can also provide valuable—and highly relevant—inbound links.

Does the website you are marketing represent a business? Business.com has listings in over 65,000 business categories. You might still think of Yellowpages.com as a telephone directory, but listings will link to a business's website. Even free agents such as freelancers and consultants have options. Industry directories abound. Sites such as MediaBistro.com link to freelance writers, editors, photographers, and others in the media business.

Better still for relevancy would be to dig down deep into your vertical area of expertise. Conduct a search of your keywords, plus a phrase such as "recommended links" or "best of the Web" or even just plain old "links." This will reveal which listings have the most link juice—for example, the online resources advocated by prestigious sites such as Breastcancer.org, Nature.com, MIT's Comparative Media Studies Program, and Forbes.com.

Many websites will fit into multiple categories, of course. That means you should, therefore, consider a variety of directories. A cultural institution that houses a restaurant, for example, might be classified under "museum" or "dining," but both features of the establishment have specific local appeal. They should also be listed in travel directories, as well as local city guides and event listings.

With scads of directories on the Web, exercising at least some judgment is in order, as well as applying common sense criteria, as follows:

■ Is the directory run by a known entity?

■ Is it a useful resource?

- Has it been around for a while (perhaps even in an offline incarnation, in the pre-Internet era, such as a local Chamber of Commerce guide or even the trusty Yellow Pages)?

- Does it contain a significant number of listings, including the "usual suspects" in the vertical area it covers? I'd certainly shy away from a New York City shopping directory that left out Bloomingdale's or Macy's.

- Does it look spammy, or contain unrelated links and content?

- Is there a clear editorial policy outlining how to be included, and what you're paying for in terms of a review? Is it designed for actual humans to use, or does it appear to be a link farm (defined in Truth 46, "Don't cultivate link farms") designed to appeal to search engines? Does the directory itself rank well in search engine listings?

- Do the links work? Lots of broken links mean an out-of-date and not maintained directory.

If it looks and smells fishy, it probably is.

Although this might sound like a long list of questions, first impressions count. If it looks and smells fishy, it probably is. Don't waste time with directories designed to separate link-hungry site owners from their money.

TRUTH

22

Using SEO PR as a
link strategy

Over the past few years, a new discipline called SEO PR has gained a strong foothold in search engine optimization, and with good reason. Putting the power of online public relations and resulting media coverage is a great strategy for building visibility on the Web and is a sound addition to link strategy as well.

News and media sites are authoritative sites—precisely the type you're looking to for inbound links to your own website. Of course, mentions in the media carry plenty of weight as third-party endorsements, or "votes" for other web properties. Well-optimized and keyword-rich press releases that go out over established wire services such as Business Wire, PR Newswire, or MarketWire are searchable by news sites. These news sites include Google News, MSN Newsbot, Yahoo! News, and Yahoo! Finance, as well as thousands of other websites that aggregate news, including Ask Jeeves News, Lycos News, Excite News, and Topix.net. Many more industry websites also pick up news releases from companies in their respective industry vertical.

It's worth noting that the two top online news portals, Yahoo! News and Google News, enjoy traffic levels that equal or exceed the top online news brands such as CNN.com or washingtonpost.com.

If you haven't already guessed, all of this adds up to instant online visibility, keyword associations, and links back to your site—and all that can occur even before the media picks up on and furthers the story (assuming, of course, the press release has enough news value to be picked up by editorial sites).

The wire services are well aware of the SEO value of news releases, and many are offering optimization services in addition to simply getting news releases "out there." Although many PR professionals still don't know about or understand the concept of SEO PR, a handful of SEO-savvy boutique PR agencies have sprung up recently. These PR agencies specialize in optimizing and releasing news for their clients with the goal of increasing search engine visibility.

How do you optimize a press release? As with a web page, you'll need to start at the top. Like human readers, news algorithms first look at the headline, then at the tease, and then at the first paragraph of text. In addition to getting keywords high on the page, it's essential to reveal the meat of the story, too. Clever, teasing, or punning headlines and summaries may work well in some contexts, but they fail when you've got only about 250 words to convey the substance of a story. This calls to mind some of the great classic headlines of *Variety*, the show business bible. "Hicks Nix Stix Pix" or "Wall Street Lays an Egg" made the history books, but fall woefully short as optimized news headlines.

It's essential to remain restrained and focused with SEO PR. It's not a license to go crazy and start spamming the wire services with irrelevant news with little or no news value. Too many keywords add up to spam, not news, and dozens upon dozens of links will likely get the release returned to you rather than out on the wires. Just as websites must above all be designed for users, not search engines, press releases must make sense to, and be written for, actual readers. Press releases that are too heavily laden with links could actually result in search engines reducing your ranking.

PR is not, of course, limited to press releases. Other authoritative content such as white papers, interviews, profiles, or original articles by company executives or experts can also be optimized and distributed online. A good example is the interactive marketing sites I ran for close to eight years. We recruited industry practitioners to author regular columns on their fields of expertise. In each byline was a link to the author's website. As ours were very authoritative editorial properties in the interactive marketing and search arenas, our authors were well aware of the "link love" and PR dividends reaped by

> Clever, teasing, or punning headlines and summaries may work well in some contexts, but they fail when you've got only about 250 words to convey the substance of a story.

> It's not a license to go crazy and start spamming the wire services with irrelevant news with little or no news value.

89

sharing their knowledge. This practice serves the dual purpose of enhancing search visibility and strengthening both of our brands.

In developing a PR strategy, don't forget to turbo-power its link potential with pictures, video, and audio. Each additional piece of media in a news release carries with it the potential for extra pick up and extra links. You can also post these multimedia files to social media sites such as YouTube, Flickr, and Facebook, further expanding both the links and quantity of relevant content surrounding them (social media SEO tactics are discussed in depth in Part VI, "Get a Social Life").

A clear advantage of SEO PR is not only the ability to reach the media (one study found that 76 percent of journalists seek press releases online), but, like all else on the Web, to also actually *become* the media and speak directly to consumers and prospects. In addition to the links an online press release can generate, the press release is now "out there" and can just as easily be found by searchers. This affords companies an avenue of speaking directly to end users that was impossible in the era when the information contained in news releases was something proprietary to the company releasing it and the media outlets re-interpreting it for public consumption.

These days, news releases themselves are readily available for public consumption.

This is good news, but it deserves to be accompanied by a note of caution. After a press release crosses the wires, it's "out there," which could damage the prospects of a hot news story being picked up by legitimate media outlets as news. Editors and journalists often consider news that has crossed the virtual wires to be already broken.

> Be judicious, and offer scoops, exclusives, or exclusive angles to media outlets that are still in the business of breaking news.

It's imperative not to go overboard with press release delirium. Editorial coverage in reputable media outlets is still a key goal of public relations strategy, as well as search engine optimization. Be judicious, and offer scoops, exclusives, or exclusive angles to media outlets that are still in the business of breaking news.

TRUTH

23

The jury is out on paid links

Looking for a gray area in SEO? You've come to the right place. Perhaps no topic in organic search optimization is more debated than that of paid links. Even defining the term can be something of a toss-up.

Very broadly put, a *paid link* (or the practice of link buying) is paying another site to links to yours. Talk about gray—weren't we just discussing paying Yahoo! $299 to express-include you in its directory a mere two Truths ago? That's a link, and it's paid, right?

Well, yes and no. Remember the adage this book keeps repeating about building websites for users, not for search engines? Search engines (Google in particular) take a dim view of buying or selling links because, in the words of Google's Matt Cutts, "If someone is buying text links to try to rank higher on search engines, they're already doing something intended more for search engines than for users."

What Cutts isn't directly saying here is that paid links also make life somewhat harder for his search engine algorithms. Hyperlinks help determine a site's reputation. Search engines would have it easier if all links were voluntary editorial "votes." Cutts argues on his blog that, "Selling links muddies the quality of link-based reputation and makes it harder for many search engines (not just Google) to return relevant results. When the Berkeley college newspaper has six online gambling links (three for casinos, two for poker, and one for bingo) on its front page, it's harder for search engines to know which links can be trusted."

Some link-buying proponents argue that although search engines can certainly make their own rules, they might also be concerned that paid links compete with their own paid contextual and search advertising programs. Search expert Chris Sherman put it rather neatly on SearchEngineLand.com: "After all, Google's primary business model is selling links, if you think about it!"

Some have said paid links that are relevant and reviewed by humans (much as display advertising is) shouldn't be subject to penalties levied by search engines against sites determined to support the practice. In fact, some search experts are even concerned that Google's online form (that can be used by anyone) to report sites using paid links to boost search rankings can be abused. Competitors or those whose own sites rank below the alleged culprits can easily be targets.

Sites that Google determines are selling links improperly can lose their capability to confer the benefit of their reputation on the other sites they link to, rendering the links functional as hyperlinks, but useless where SEO is concerned.

Told you this topic was complicated!

Meanwhile, a quick search on any of the major search engines will turn up no shortage of companies eager to act as link brokers. Most pledge, of course, that their practices are fully ethical, relevant, and above-board. Some sites are known to auction links to the highest bidder. Google's bottom line on ethical paid links is that they should contain the "nofollow" tag (discussed in Truth 28, "Putting the kibosh on link love with nofollow links"), which prevent search engine crawlers from following, and hence counting, the link.

By now, a few highly opinionated pros and cons regarding link buying should have begun to emerge, such as the following:

- Search engines frown on the practice.

- Experts disagree on how, when, under what circumstances, and even if links should be bought or sold.

- Buying just the right link may drive high-quality traffic to your site—search engines be damned!

> Buying links?
> That's advertising,
> not organic SEO!

- Buying links? That's advertising, not organic SEO!

- You put a lot of time and effort into building links—so in a sense, you "pay" for them anyway.

- Buying links is fine so long as there's disclosure, just as with any other form of advertising.

Clearly, buying links is no playing field for the uninformed. It's also one of those situations in which being informed seems to hinder as much as it might help, given that buying links can offer benefits, but can also potentially penalize websites.

Clearly, buying links is no playing field for the uninformed.

The best advice when buying (or selling) links is concerned is likely not to make the practice a cornerstone of any SEO initiative. There are too many, much more important areas to focus on first: relevant, optimized content; intelligent site architecture; meta data; and of course, developing and maintaining a strong, ongoing editorial linking strategy.

TRUTH

24

Share and share alike:
Reciprocal linking

I'll link to you if you link to me....

A reciprocal link is pretty much just what it sounds like: Two (and sometimes more) websites agree to link to one another to boost traffic, as well as to increase search engine visibility. This type of linking can also be referred to as "link swaps," "link exchanges," and "link partners."

If you were an early web user, you might recall "web rings." Sites that all dealt with a similar topic created these rings, explicitly recommending that their visitors visit these other, similar sites. That's one kind of reciprocal linking.

A more modern example of reciprocal linking is one website that specializes in traditional Chinese recipes and cooking techniques exchanging links with another site, which sells hard-to-find Asian ingredients and cooking utensils. These two sites are very obviously complementary, and not at all competitive with one another. (A major reason for the demise of web rings was competition, when online advertising heated up.)

Clearly, the users of the recipe and cooking website can benefit from having a source for the tools necessary to create the recipes. The utensil and ingredient seller's audience can certainly benefit from knowing how to properly use the ingredients and implements they can buy on the second site. (In fact, this knowledge might actually help to increase sales.) The two sites agree to a reciprocal link. In essence, they're "voting" for one another, or vouching for one another's credibility and relevance. This can help increase traffic for both sites, underscore both sites' relevancy in search algorithms (Chinese/Asian cooking), make both sites more crawlable (thanks to additional inbound links), and help to raise the profiles of both sites in search engine rankings.

Everyone wins.

Reciprocal linking is, in the best sense, a win-win scenario: more traffic, more relevance, and more search visibility. Some sites even take it upon themselves to link to direct competitors, calculating that the benefits of relevance and search visibility outweigh the obvious disadvantages.

As with other types of linking, quality matters just as much as quantity. There's certainly nothing stopping a company that manufactures snow tires from linking to a site concerned only with Asian delicacies—but why would it bother? Such a link wouldn't count on the relevancy scorecard. (In fact, it could even hurt.) Reciprocal linking isn't willy-nilly. It involves an ongoing commitment of time, research, and dialogue with other sites.

In other words, the concept is simple. The execution requires plenty of commitment!

An obvious place to start with reciprocal linking is with the search engines themselves, of course. Look for sites focused on content areas that complement your own field of expertise. Depending on your own website, this could vary widely—site-wide, section-by-section, or even on a page-by-page basis.

Step two entails visiting those sites that come up as likely prospects. If you're that Asian cooking utensil seller, a recipe site with just one or two Chinese dishes featured isn't as likely a reciprocal link partner as those featuring only (or primarily) Chinese, Korean, Japanese, and Thai dishes. And bear in mind you're looking not only for sites that you're hoping will link to you, but also sites you are willing to link to—essentially, to endorse—from your own website. Once again, quality counts.

> ...you're looking not only for sites that you're hoping will link to you, but also sites you are willing to link to—essentially, to endorse—from your own website.

Make a list of the likely candidates and link to them from your website. Only after doing so should you compose a short, personalized note (use the webmaster's or publisher's name whenever possible). Take care that the note includes a positive remark about their site. If you can't find that one positive thing, drop the site from your list and don't bother to get in touch. If you can't provide them with a reason why you linked, why on earth would they bother to link back? Provide the URL of the page that links to their site and suggest very specifically where they might link back to you from one of their pages. Develop a schedule to follow up on inquiries, perhaps even by phone or by mail. (E-mails are easy to overlook or ignore.) A good link from a quality site isn't guaranteed, but it's worth that extra bit of effort.

As with all things in SEO, when there's a right way to do things, there's often a wrong way. A very wrong way! Link exchange websites exist to continually and actively exchange links with one another, often via processes that are almost entirely automated. You've been warned. Often these schemes connect you to link farms (see Truth 46, "Don't cultivate link farms") at worst, and at best utterly irrelevant sites. At best, this benefits your own site not a bit. At worst, involvement in this sort of scheme can get your site banned from search engines altogether. Don't do it!

> As with all things in search engine optimization, when there's a right way to do things, there's often a wrong way.

Reciprocal content linking

Although a link might be the end goal, reciprocal links (and any other type on links on a web page) require context and relevancy. So instead of laser focus on just the link, consider how that link can be presented. Often, relevant content is the answer. Swapping articles, how-tos, or other helpful content that contains links between sites just may be the ticket. Let's go back to our Asian food sites. The recipe site might have an article about "The Five Must-Have Tools for Chinese Cooking." The ingredient and utensil site, meanwhile, could feature helpful articles on "Recipes Using Oyster Sauce" or "Seasoning and Caring for a New Wok."

This approach has the hallmarks of the best SEO strategy: highly relevant content written for users, but with links, keywords, and phrases that make it search-engine-friendly. Combining strong, relevant content with reciprocal linking makes a win-win strategy even more successful.

TRUTH

25

Ads are links, too

Paying for links is certainly a gray area (see Truth 23, "The jury is out on paid links"), partially because search engines frown upon the practice, and partially because any paid link is regarded as advertising, rather than as "pure" organic search optimization.

Yet because virtually every online ad contains a link back to the advertiser's web, product, or brand site does present an unavoidable fact that can affect search optimization: These paid links can and do affect search rankings. Paid advertisements can, therefore, be considered to be part of a linking strategy. This, in turn, makes them worthy of consideration in a discussion of SEO.

It's at least in part (if not wholly) for this reason that many leading advertising-supported websites—including many that cover search engine marketing and advertising—carry "sponsored by" ads on their homepages or in other site sections. Companies offering products and services related to SEO and SEM are naturally eager to have links to their own sites from some of the leading editorial properties in the industry, and are, therefore, willing to buy their way into guaranteed, long-term links back to their offerings.

The same holds true, of course, for editorial properties in other vertical business industries. SEO has, in short, established a new reason for buying advertising or sponsorships on relevant, high-quality, third-party sites. The reason? A prominent link from a quality website back to the advertiser's own site is too valuable to ignore.

The same holds true of sites that sell directory listings, as well as enhanced and expanded listings in existing directories. Think of your local Yellow Pages as a corollary. All the locksmiths in a given city or neighborhood might be listed in that directory, but some locksmiths find value in paying for a larger or more prominent ad with an additional phone number (the Yellow Pages equivalent of a link) to highlight their business listing, offering, and relevance to that particular segment of the directory.

> Buying online ads wholly or in part for the value of the link is certainly a tactic to consider when plotting a link strategy.

Buying online ads wholly or in part for the value of the link is certainly a tactic to consider when plotting a link strategy. It's important to bear in mind, however, that links in ads still qualify as paid links in the strictest sense of the term. As such, the possibility that their "link juice" is discounted, discredited, or diluted by the search engines because of the fact that they do appear in ads does exist. Very possibly, search engine algorithms can "read" this information based on the placement of ads on the publisher's page, or the fact that such ads might appear under a heading such as "site sponsors," and thereby be partially or wholly discredited as valid links. A very small handful of publishers might also place links within the "nofollow" attribute (see Truth 28, "Putting the kibosh on link love with nofollow links") so that the link's target is not "counted" toward search engine ranking.

> Publishers, for obvious reasons, are much more focused on keeping their advertisers happy—at least, until Google starts paying their bills.

Although using the nofollow attribute is the method Google prefers, the sites and publishers that have adopted the technique are few and far between. Publishers, for obvious reasons, are much more focused on keeping their advertisers happy—at least, until Google starts paying their bills.

Even when ads are purchased purely as advertising rather than as part of a link-building strategy, it's worthwhile taking the significance of the links in an ad into account. If the link is embedded in a text ad, that text should be relevant to the offer and the landing page, rather than a more generic "Interested? Click here for more information."

There's no reason to throw SEO learnings out the window when working with other aspects and channels of interactive marketing and media. So, even when an ad is only an ad, remember that it's also a link, too. Why not wring out all the link juice you can?

> ...even when an ad is only an ad, remember that it's also a link, too. Why not wring out all the link juice you can?

101

TRUTH

26

Build your site in a good neighborhood

Location, location, location. This adage holds true for more than just real estate. It applies just as well to the "neighborhood" in which a website resides. When it comes to search engine optimization, search engines will judge you by the company you keep—and rank you accordingly. Bad, discourteous, and unruly neighbors can bump you down the rankings. In a worst-case scenario, they can wipe you right out of search engine results.

What constitutes a "neighborhood" among the billions and billions of sites on the Internet? Just as real-world neighborhoods consists of communities linked together by common networks of streets, roads, fences, boundaries, highways, railroads, and pathways, online neighborhoods, too, are intricate systems of links.

> When it comes to search engine optimization, search engines will judge you by the company you keep—and rank you accordingly.

And just as living next door to a derelict building, crack house, or noisy neighbor would reflect badly on your own real estate values (no matter how scrupulously you maintained your own property), virtual proximity to bad neighbors has much the same effect on search engine rankings.

Here's what Google has to say about SEO real estate:

```
"Avoid links to web spammers or 'bad
neighborhoods' on the web, as your own
ranking may be affected adversely by those
links."
```

So, what's a bad Web neighborhood? Any site that uses underhanded or unethical tactics to try to increase its site's rankings or mislead its visitors can be classified as a bad neighbor.

These dirty tricks include the following:

- Cloaking
- Spammers
- Installing viruses or malware

- Free-for-all link pages

- Link farms

- Keyword stuffing

- Duplicate content (or lack of any original content)

- Hidden text and links

- Doorway pages

- Deceptive titles

- Machine-generated pages

- Copyright violators

- Breaking other guidelines

For a more in-depth discussion of these misdeeds, see Part IX, "Don't Be Evil."

All these infractions can result in a site being penalized or quarantined by Google—as well as the other search engines. Link to these bad apples, and you're guilty, at least in part by association. Like real-world bad neighborhoods, online danger zones are often recognized by a propensity toward drugs, sex for sale, gambling, and other illicit-bordering-on-illegal activities.

When in doubt as to whether a site to which you're interested in linking is considered a bad neighborhood, a simple search engine check can help reveal how the search engines themselves regard the property. Enter this protocol: site:companyurlhere. If the domain doesn't show up in the search results, it's probably because the site is question has been penalized. Because you're judged by the company you keep (by search engines as well as visitors to your own site), it's probably best not to link.

> Link to these bad apples, and you're guilty, at least in part by association.

Don't lose too much sleep over this if you've got an above-board, ethical linking policy. The odd bad link isn't going to torpedo all your search engine optimization efforts and knock you out of the search ballpark for all time. What search engines, specifically Google, are most concerned with are linking patterns. As Google's Adam Lasnik put it on a WebmasterWorld.com discussion board: "Our algorithms are tuned to look for patterns of 'egregious' linking behavior—both on individual sites and in the aggregate."

A big part of determining whether a neighborhood is good is not only learning more about your neighbors, but also keeping your own yard clean. Is the lawn clean and tidy? Is the grass mowed, and are the flowers blooming? Or is the front porch littered with the rusting shell of a discarded refrigerator next to a torn and sagging sofa?

In other words, it's important to conduct routine maintenance on your own links. Too many links to 404 pages (that is, web pages or sites that have moved, or no longer exist) are not only contextually irrelevant and not helpful to visitors, but also can mount in number over time and, unchecked, create problems. So, although not linking to sites of ill repute should be common sense, it's also important to keep your own home tidy and regularly check links, updating or eliminating them if necessary.

Keeping your own site neat and tidy makes the Web a better neighborhood for everybody, and it certainly won't hurt your search rankings, either.

TRUTH
27

Blogs are a terrific link strategy

Want to get into the fast lane of building a solid link strategy? Think blogs. Blogs have soared in popularity over recent years, and with good reason. They're an efficient, easy, and low cost way to communicate and publish ideas. Otherwise put, blogs are an excellent way to generate high-quality content, generally around a specific unifying theme.

Sound familiar? It should, given that high-quality, keyword-rich content is also one of the primary components of search engine optimization. It's no small wonder that Google acquired Blogger, a popular blogging platform, early in the evolution of the channel.

There is a panoply of reasons to integrate blogging into marketing and communications initiatives. This is evidenced by the fact that blogs have been embraced by the marketing community. Blogs have another recognized and relevant function where SEO is concerned: Blogs are an invaluable tool for building up links, both in- and outbound.

Blogs are literally built to attract search engine crawlers and spiders. Their architecture and design are structured for clear navigation, with every page set up to link back to other primary pages. It is no surprise that in recent years, many successful and profitable publishers have built editorial products entirely on commercial blog platforms.

Blogs are literally built to attract search engine crawlers and spiders.

A blog can easily be set up to repeat target keywords in the titles of individual posts, category names, URLs, in tags, and in the links that appear as footers on each post. The RSS feeds generated by a blog are automatically picked up by search engines at regular intervals, as are the pages themselves. (By the way, feeds should be registered with the blog search engine, technorati.com.)

You don't need to post frequently, but every time you do, it's like strewing spider-bait, as far as the search engines are concerned. Blogs are very easily crawlable—and therein lies powerful linking advantage.

Blogs contain several different types of links. Not all of them have the same degree of link-love power, but all are highly useful in enhancing a link-building strategy.

You don't need to post frequently, but every time you do, it's like strewing spider-bait, as far as the search engines are concerned.

Blogrolls

Many blogs feature a blogroll on the homepage. A *blogroll* is a list of blogs recommended or endorsed by the author(s). Remember how links are equated to "votes" or "endorsements" by search engines? This is a literal opportunity to do just that, while contextualizing the content of your own blog. For example, if you're blogging about cars, and your blogroll links to 10 or 12 other automotive-related blogs, you're not only imparting link love on your blogging colleagues; at the same time, you're giving Yahoo!, Google, and MSN a clearer idea of your own content niche.

Supporting commercial entities

An increasing number of blogs support businesses, organizations, events, or any number of commercial entities. This isn't just to boost exposure and visibility on the communications front, but also because blogs can dramatically help increase the search visibility of the sites they support or are related to. This can be achieved in the blog's tagline, like so:

```
The XYZ Blog
by John Doe, CEO of XYZ Corp.
```

In this example, "XYZ Corp." links to the homepage of the company, and perhaps the author "John Doe" links to his corporate bio on the site. When setting up authors on a blog platform, the person or persons authorized to post entries can associate an URL with his or her name—yet more link potential.

Links in blog posts

The most potent link juice blogs can offer are the links in actual posts. When writing blog content, link early and link often, particularly to other blogs. Bloggers are highly aware of and sensitive to the power of link love (or should we call it link karma?) and will often reward inbound links with links back to your blog without being asked to return the favor. In the case of a blog that exists to promote another website or business, remember that spiders crawl links, and all this additional linking serves the purpose of creating additional pathways—some direct, and some indirect—back to the target of the optimization effort.

As with any and all web content, remember that you're not blogging for search engines. You're blogging for human readers, and having a solid content strategy for a blog is of paramount importance. That's how you're going to get others to read and link to it in the first place. Your first order of business should be to produce solid content, not to attract or to play tricks on search engines. With that in mind, remember that being topical or even controversial is likely to attract more attention, and therefore more links.

> As with any and all web content, remember that you're not blogging for search engines. You're blogging for human readers....

There are some aspects of blog linking that you shouldn't lose too much sleep over. Trackbacks add a bit of link juice, but due to spamming, not as much as they once did. That said, trackbacks provide a very useful function by letting you know who's linking to your posts. This can result in discussion and potentially new links down the road.

Links in blog post comments have also fallen prey to spammers, and are, therefore, of only limited link value (and sometimes none at all, depending on the blog platform used). However like trackbacks, they open avenues for further communication and dialog.

And anyway, you'd never comment on a blog post just because you were looking to add another link to your site, would you? Of course you wouldn't. You'd comment because you had something valuable, interesting, or useful to say!

TRUTH

28

Putting the kibosh on link love with nofollow links

As blogging has risen in popularity, so has blog spam. Bloggers often load blog entries with links and comment spam. The goal, of course, is to link to other websites and pages to boost those external sites' link juice and to boost search engine PageRank. In other words, the system of using hyperlinks to "vote" for the usefulness or relevancy of sites has been abused—often egregiously—by spammers hawking dubious wares and services.

Enter the "nofollow" tag, introduced by Google in 2005. The promise of the nofollow tag was not to stop spam (which itself is all but unstoppable), but rather to remove any of the link love value in a link in blog comments. The nofollow tag tells search engines that the link shouldn't "count" as a vote of confidence in whatever page or site to which the link points. That's why some SEOs refer to the nofollow tag as a "link condom."

Adding the nofollow tag to a hyperlink is supposed to effectively eradicate any value that link may confer on the page or site to which it points.

> ...some SEOs refer to the nofollow tag as a "link condom."

Nofollow is baked into the Google-owned Blogger platform by default, as well as most other blogging platforms, including the WordPress platform. (There are also workarounds for the technically inclined.) Numerous social bookmarking and photo-sharing websites also use nofollow tags for outgoing links. These include Digg.com, Furl, Propeller.com (formerly Netscape.com), Yahoo! My Web 2.0, YouTube, and Technorati Favs. Wikipedia also adopted the tag for its outbound links.

Because Google frowns on paid links, it also came up with another recommendation for using the nofollow tag. Google argued that site publishers who sell links solely for PageRank value were deliberately trying to stick it to the system. So, many publishers began to use nofollow tags to indicate to Google that they weren't adding links or ads to their sites solely for the value of the link juice.

Some site owners even use nofollow tags internally. This directs search engine spiders not to follow internal links on their sites to pages such as the privacy policy, or "About Us" or "Contact Us" pages. The value of this practice is hotly debated. After all, there are searchers out there looking for precisely that information.

After Google introduced nofollow, Yahoo! and MSN said they would support the standard (although each search engine approaches nofollow differently), whereas Ask.com ignores it completely. Google claims not to follow links designated as nofollow at all, although this claim is disputed by many SEOs. However, Google does not index the linked-to page. Of course, it's wholly possible that the page in question was already in Google's index. Similarly, Yahoo! and MSN respect the attribute and exclude nofollow links from their ranking calculations.

Nofollow is an imperfect tool. There's no across-the-board agreement on how to use it. Certainly it's helped to stop the PageRank effect of some blog comment spam, but it's not as if it's stopped that particular genre of spam altogether (as any blogger sporting a comment feature will certainly affirm). Nofollow has also been criticized for discouraging comments from qualified professionals and opinion-leaders. Often, these qualified professionals don't bother to add insightful feedback to blog entries because the link won't pay off in link love. Google would like link sellers to use nofollow, but the practice is too widespread and non-transparent for any real kind of implementation in that regard.

So, use nofollow judiciously. One practical way it's often implemented by site owners is in instances of linking to competitive sites, or information about competitors. Although the information linked to may be valuable or relevant to site visitors, at least you're not helping boost the competition's PageRank with the link.

> Nofollow is an imperfect tool. There's no across-the-board agreement on how to use it.

Bottom line: The rel="nofollow" attribute is here to stay; a few more years of testing and a few dozen search engine algorithms updates from now, it will likely have far different value than it holds today. Nofollow is an interesting tag that started on a simple-enough mission: to rid the world of spammers. It's evolved into a tool to be used wisely and tested consistently.

Nofollow is an interesting tag that started on a simple-enough mission: to rid the world of spammers.

Finally, bear in mind that nofollow does not render content invisible, preventing search engines from indexing it or users from finding it. If you have a need to block search engines from finding content on your own site, see Truth 51, "Sometimes you don't want to be found," in the final section of this book.

TRUTH

29

Search is going vertical

Thought you only had to optimize your site for Google, Yahoo!, MSN, and perhaps as an afterthought, Ask. com? Think again.

The Internet is a network of billions and billions of websites and pages, and the major search engines search all of them (or at least, all of them that are accessible to the search engines). As the Web grows, so do search engine indices. That can be a pretty good thing. Good, at least until you're searching for something very specific and are overwhelmed by a panoply of results, many or most of which are irrelevant to the original query.

Say you're planning to go bass fishing for vacation. You navigate over to Yahoo! and search for "bass." The first page of results refers to fishing but dedicates even more space to bass guitars, Bass shoes, and Bass Ale. But over at FishSeekers.com, a search engine dedicated to all things fishing-related, you get all bass fishing results, all the time, on that same "bass" search query.

Specialized search engines (increasingly called vertical search engines) don't scour the entire Web looking for everything. Instead, they send out their crawlers to specific databases that contain information about a particular (and often very specific) topic or field of interest. This might include fishing, shopping, medicine, travel, jobs, real estate, veterinarians, song lyrics, and specific business channels. The list is endless...and growing. There are search engines for the websites related to human rights, cats, cartoons, UFOs, real-time flight tracking, Macintosh computers, restaurants, kids' sites, classified ads, automotive, software, games, real estate, law, health for consumers, and health for medical professionals. There are search engines that look for content only on the mobile Web, or seek out only video and/or audio.

And that's just for starters.

The major search engines are getting into the game, too. On Google's homepage searches, search results can be narrowed considerably to categories such as Images, Maps, News, and Shopping. Click on the "more" tab, and you're greeted with still more categories: blogs, video, groups, books, scholar, and finance. If that weren't enough, there's an "even more" tab where you can search for patents, products, search within specific topics, or even get help building a search tool for your own specific brand of community.

Vertical search is critically important to website owners, particularly those operating commercial sites, because of the mindset of the searchers who use them. When someone searches for "iPod" on a general search engine, they may be looking for how-to tips, technical specifications, or repair information. Maybe they're just trying to grab a photo of a pink iPod for a project they're working on. But when that same user looks for "iPod" on a shopping search engine, their intent becomes much, much clearer—and that much more interesting to online iPod merchants. By the same token, a web search for "France" could be a student working on a term paper, someone needing a map, or someone with an interest in politics or even French cuisine.

Vertical search helps reveal the searcher's motivations and intent....

A search for "France" on a travel search engine?

Well, you get the idea. Vertical search helps reveal the searcher's motivations and intent in a field where technology and algorithms have made enormous strides, but not to the point at which they're reading searchers' minds.

An equally difficult challenge to address is how do you optimize for vertical search when there are thousands (or tens, or even hundreds of thousands) of specialized search engines out there, each one different, and each applying to only a teeny-tiny subsection of what's out there on the Web?

Beyond the all-too-obvious response: If you have high-quality, popular, vertically focused content on your site, these search engines will find you. There's no set of one-size-fits-all answers to optimizing for vertical search. That's the bad news.

There's no set of one-size-fits-all answers to optimizing for vertical search.

The good news is that there are certainly guidelines to follow, particularly in several of the most important and broadest vertical categories—and these are the ones a majority of searchers are using. There might be more vertical search engines out there than you can shake a USB stick at, but overall searchers are concentrating on more popular categories, such as shopping, local, news, blogs, and health. That's why these are the vertical categories featured on the major web search engines.

Otherwise put, there may be a pizza search engine out there somewhere. If there is, I don't know about it. (And I'm not going to look for it, either.) Your average pizza searcher has something more specific in mind, such as she wants a pizza delivered. Now. In New York City. Preferably, in or near the zip code 10019.

Forget pizza search. This is exactly where local search comes into the picture.

Truths 30–33 explain how to determine what major vertical search categories a website belongs to and how to optimize for those major vertical search categories.

TRUTH

30

Everyone is local somewhere

As far back as 2004, local search accounted for up to 25 percent of commercial activity on the Web, according to a Kelsey Group study. No wonder large and small players alike have been striving to build a better local search mousetrap. Of all the large and small search verticals out there, local is the fastest-growing and, probably, most important.

It's not hard to understand why. A dentist in Des Moines may have a Web presence, but it's unlikely he'll be filling cavities in Cleveland. If your drain clogs in Denver, a plumber in Pittsburgh isn't what you need now. The major search engines know this, in fact. Various geo-location technologies are baked into their algorithms. So when someone with a toothache in Des Moines searches for a "dentist," one of the Big Three search engines is likely to figure out where she is (IP addresses are one indicator) and shove that local dentist's site to the top of the results.

Pretty neat, right?

Well, it works if the search engine knows about the dentist in Des Moines. Therein lies much of the wisdom when it comes to optimizing for local search: defining locality (where is your company located and what area do you serve?).

It's not only local service providers, shops, and tradesmen who benefit from local search optimization. So, too, do national retailers. You don't just want to visit Wal-Mart; you want to visit the nearest Wal-Mart. You don't order a pizza from Domino's corporate headquarters, but you do want to order from the Domino's in your neighborhood. Local search is important to every business, organization, and service with a localized customer base—or bases.

It's a pity more businesses don't know about and take advantage of local search. Local search can level the playing field considerably between large national businesses and small local providers. Given a degree of search savvy and a Web presence, a neighborhood flower shop could have just as much

> Local search can level the playing field considerably between large national businesses and small local providers.

visibility and clout as a nationwide florist such as FTD or 1-800-Flowers. It's a matter not only of knowing how to play the game, but also of knowing the game exists in the first place.

A down-and-dirty (as well as highly effective) technique to optimize for local search is not to rely on a single "Contact" page for local information. A local business can add a footer to every single page of its website that contains its street address, city, state, zip code, and local phone number, including area code. Quite possibly, it's appropriate to use a degree of location in title tags as well—for example, Smith, Brown, & Jones Law Firm, Dallas/Forth Worth, TX.

Locally oriented keywords and phrases are also critical, and should take into account the various terms people use to refer to localities, which can be broad as well as specific. Here's a hypothetical example with local keywords highlighted:

> *Chicago*'s premier locksmith serving all regions of the *Chicagoland* area. We offer locksmith services in *Lincoln Park*, *Lakeview*, *Wicker Park*, the *South Side*, *Old Town*, and the *Near Northside of Chicago*. We also serve the *Chicago* suburbs of *Evanston*, *Glencoe*, and *Highland Park*.

No one in the great Chicago area ever refers to their region as "northern Illinois." But if they did, you can bet our fictitious locksmith would have cobbled the state's name into his keywords as well. He's betting on the fact that his customers aren't just searching for a "chicago locksmith" in a town that big, but are winnowing down their searches to a more localized level, such as neighborhood.

Also bear in mind that local is as local does. The preceding chapter mentioned a New Yorker in Zip Code 10019 who wanted to order a pizza. New York is a large, but concentrated, urban area. Few residents of the city would be willing to travel more than a handful of blocks for a pizza. In Montana or New Mexico, by contrast, a customer may be willing to drive miles for the same pie. Yahoo! and Google Local know this. Both services sort results by distance.

When coming up with a local optimization plan, it's critically important to understand what local is for the area in question.

A first step in local search optimization is ensuring that your business is listed with the major search engines, as well as with the Internet Yellow Pages (IYP). The IYP is the source of much of the local data used by search engines, as well as other online directories and listing services. Do they have the correct information? Is your listing linked to your website? Businesses with multiple locations in a single metro area can benefit from having separate directory listings for each and every location.

Don't overlook local listings on popular directory services, such as Zagat, Citysearch, Yelp, Superpages, Judy's Book, Yahoo! Local, travel guides, regional websites such as Boston.com and Nola.com (both run by major newspapers), ShopLocal, Chambers of Commerce, and local trade associations and other business groups.

For many local businesses, user-generated content and star ratings are a critical component of search results. The more—well, the more positive ones—the merrier. Ratings and reviews create additional relevant content associated with a business or listing, deeper descriptions, third-party authority, and can often be sorted by rating.

There's no reason not to get the ball rolling by asking friends and family to begin reviewing or rating your business. A hairdressing salon in my neighborhood has a sign on the counter politely asking clients to add their comments about the business to Citysearch. In addition to creating greater search visibility and content, third-party reviews amount to a form of word-of-mouth marketing, one of the most persuasive and influential types of persuasion out there. It's worth spending time developing ratings and reviews, particularly in a local context.

> Third-party reviews amount to a form of word-of-mouth marketing, one of the most persuasive and influential types of persuasion out there.

Further emphasize locality by adding a page (or perhaps adding to your contact page) of detailed directions for finding your business or office location. Write these out in detail, like so:

Lakehurst Flower Shop is near the Wakeland
County Shopping Mall in the Bellevue
neighborhood of Lakehurst, MD. To find
us, drive west on Hometown Drive past the
Grangeville Civic Center, then turn left
on Elm Street. You'll find us at 425 Oak
Street, Suite 201, Lakehurst, MD, 12345.

Add a link to a map service (Google, Yahoo!, MSN,
MapQuest, and so on). And when linking to the directions
page, "click here for directions" isn't good enough. Instead,
use "click here for directions to our Lakehurst flower store."

TRUTH

31

Get listed to get vertical

As discussed in Truth 21, "Building links through online directories," directory listings aren't only an important link-building strategy. Listings in appropriate vertically oriented directories help to contextualize the focus, content, and scope of a website (and the business or organization that it represents). This listing can, in turn, help to contextualize and promote the site in vertical search listings.

We looked at this briefly in the last truth, in which we discussed how inclusion in directories such as Zagat, Citysearch, Yelp, Superpages, Judy's Book, Yahoo! Local, travel guides, About.com, or regional websites, such as Boston.com, could help highlight a site's local value and boost its ranking in local search results, while at the same time provide important clues regarding the context and relevancy of the site in question. Say a business is called "China Garden." Is it a garden? A park? Is it a restaurant? A Chinese restaurant? A Chinese restaurant specializing in Szechuan cuisine in the Buckhead neighborhood of Atlanta, GA?

Search engines glean much of this kind of information (as, by extension, do searchers)—to such a great extent that online directories, which are searchable, are confused with search engines by some, and are even considered search engines by others. Broadly put, the fundamental difference between a directory and a "real" search engine is that the search engine is wholly automated and technology-based, whereas a directory is edited and reviewed by actual human beings.

> [a] search engine is wholly automated and technology-based, whereas a directory is edited and reviewed by actual human beings....

This degree of editorial selectivity generally imparts a degree of quality, authority, and relevance that can exceed organic search engine results. This editorial selectivity also helps individual sites to rank higher in organic results by benefit of the links provided in the directories. Additionally, the text accompanying directory listings is often written, or at least vetted for content and accuracy, by these human editors so the messaging comes across as less "marketing-y." These editors generally visit the site to check its content and overall quality, and to ensure that listings appear in the appropriate category.

Because of directories' hierarchical structure, they often provide a systematic, orderly way for searchers to peruse the listings they contain. Generally, directories can searched by business vertical, by location, by services provided, and so on. For searchers, this can be much faster and more efficient than sifting through all the Chinese restaurants that come up in a search of the World Wide Web. Or in another of a myriad of examples, real estate listings might be sorted by two-bedroom, detached houses with gardens and garages within a specific zip code.

Because directories tend to be neat, orderly, organized, authoritative, and aligned around clearly defined topics, search engines like them. A lot. Search engine crawlers often use directories as a first stop in their quest for locating quality sites to add to their indices. They follow the links on directory sites to the listed websites, and then continue further and deeper in their quest to mine information. This is why directories were also discussed in depth in Part IV, "The Truth About Links."

> Because directories tend to be neat, orderly, organized, authoritative, and aligned around clearly-defined topics, search engines like them. A lot.

In addition to getting listed in general web directories such as Yahoo!'s or DMOZ (even from a purely SEO standpoint, it's often worth considering paying a fee to do so), it's worth the time and effort to seek out relevant vertical directories for your website and the products, services, or content it represents. Submitting a new listing is fast and relatively painless, and is often free or for a very small fee.

If it's worth submitting a site to a directory, it's worth paying attention to each individual directory's submission guidelines—and then following them!

If you're only allowed to submit to one category, submit to the most appropriate one. Don't try to fool or trick the editors into including your site multiple times. If site descriptions are limited to 200 characters, or 100 words, stay within those limits and make every character in the copy count. (Perhaps you can even include some important keywords?)

Relevant copy that fits the category not only serves your site better, but also makes the editor's job easier. "A really great website" just isn't as helpful as "car, truck, and van rentals in California, Oregon, and Washington state." Often, a directory requires listings to be factual and neutral rather than "sales-y." But be careful to differentiate your site to give editors a reason to include it. If it sounds the same as others in the category, why should they bother? Emphasize the site's value to visitors.

> Be careful to differentiate your site to give editors a reason to include it. If it sounds the same as others in the category, why should they bother?

Many SEOs are careful to tweak description copy for individual directories. When each submission is ever so slightly individualized, it's easier to track which directory submissions are making it into search results on the different search engines.

TRUTH

32

Optimize off-site searches

YouTube. Craigslist. eBay. Wikipedia, Flickr. What do these sites—together with a host of others—have in common? All, in their own way, can be considered search engines.

Yet none spider the Web, nor create an index of content outside of what resides on their own respective databases. Also, none exist with the primary purpose of sending their visitor traffic away, as do Yahoo!, Google, Ask, and MSN.

These, and similar sites, also operate to some extent like directories. But in behind-the-scenes conversations with these companies' founders and managers, you're likely to hear some very interesting comments. "We're the largest shopping search engine in the world," an eBay executive once told me. And you thought it was an auction site! It's no small wonder eBay acquired Craigslist, the website that's long been giving traditional classified ad providers a run for their money (online as well as off). It's also no surprise that Google snapped up YouTube, where people fritter away hours searching videos they're interested in and "video snacking."

Zillow, if you haven't heard of it, is a powerful real estate search engine that not only provides listings of available properties in designated areas, but also all kinds of other sales and property valuation information. Like its better-known peers in the real estate listings vertical, Zillow is navigated primarily via search.

You might call this category of sites directories, specialized or vertical search engines, but for the purposes of optimizing content on them, it really doesn't matter. As with the "real" search engines, you can buy ads on most of these websites. But what really matters to most of the sellers, buyers, browsers, and users of these sites, commercial or otherwise, is the ability to find what they're searching for.

It's easy for SEOs to get so caught up in optimizing their own sites that they neglect the extra effort and push it takes to optimize their off-site efforts.

It's easy for SEOs to get so caught up in optimizing their own sites that they neglect the extra effort and push it takes to optimize their off-site efforts. With search the de facto way to navigate the Web, not to mention many of the major sites on it, this is a grave oversight.

The reasons to represent products, brands, services, or other offerings on websites other than your own are manifold. The first and most obvious is it broadens reach. Companies may, for example, post open positions on their own websites, but the pool of potential candidates is obviously deeper when jobs are listed in classified ads in local newspaper sites or on Craigslist. Perhaps you sell products. Listings on eBay, or even an eBay or Amazon merchant store, can put your wares in front of plenty of additional eyeballs.

An off-site presence, whether through listings or advertising, can confer the added advantage of inbound links back to your site from sites carrying links back to yours. Some, such as Wikipedia, are highly valuable and sought-after. Wikipedia listings have begun to appear at or near the top of Google's search results as the online encyclopedia grows in reach, influence, and credibility.

That's why wise search optimizers don't just focus on how their own web properties perform in major search engine rankings. They're also careful to optimize their presence elsewhere as well.

The principles of off-site optimization don't significantly differ from getting your own site ranked in search engines. The overriding goal of off-site optimization remains fundamentally the same as with search engine optimization: Get found when searchers are looking for what you've got. The potential bonus is adding a jolt or two of visibility by means of link juice to your own website or property.

...wise search optimizers don't just focus on how their own web properties perform in major search engine rankings. They're also careful to optimize their presence elsewhere as well.

TRUTH

33

Universal search and personalized search

Just because you are number one in search engine results today, doesn't mean you will be number one tomorrow. Search rankings don't just rise and fall because of the routine tweaks and updates major search engines are constantly making to their algorithms and indices. They fluctuate because the nature of search is changing as search engines extend their reach for what many consider to be the brass ring in the search engine's game: searcher intent.

For example, let say someone searches for "123 Main Street, Mytown, USA 12345." A couple of years ago, the top result on Google would probably have been a business at that address. Today, the top result for an address search is likely to be a graphic: a Google map with that particular location starred.

Search for "beatles sgt pepper," and Google guesses you're looking to buy the album. The top results link to the product on Amazon, Circuit City, and CD Universe. Searching for "indiana jones" produces a link to a video trailer for the most recent film in the series, "Indiana Jones and the Kingdom of the Crystal Skull," together with a box in which a searcher can input his or her zip code for local theaters and show times. Current topics in the news, such as "george w bush" or "global warming" deliver news stories as the top results, accompanied by photographs.

Welcome to universal search, in which combinations of vertical search results, together with news, local, video, and image results, are beginning to appear at the top of the page by default. This effort by search engines to anticipate and meet searcher intent (for example, if I'm searching for a film, it's because I want to see it; if I'm searching for an address, it's because I want to find the location) is one of the many ways search is irrevocably changing.

Inevitably, universal search is changing search engine optimization, too. Optimizing a site, or the bits and pieces of content and media on a web property, now has different and shifting implications. First and foremost, it's more important than ever to pay attention to optimizing media files such as video, graphics, and photos. It's now wholly possible that videos, graphics, and photos might appear in the top results in lieu of a link to an actual website.

Universal search also means being number one isn't what it used to be. Yours might be the top-ranked website when search results show up for a given query, but the top-ranked site no longer necessarily appears in that coveted number-one position in search results. Moreover, because that top result (or set of results) may occupy a large swath of search result real estate (such as a map, a photo, or an image), the top-ranked site is further down the page. Results that formerly appeared on page one in lower-ranked positions can be pushed to the second or third page of search results, making them less evident to searchers.

Search algorithms aren't the only thing changing. The entire nature of search is in a state of constant upheaval and evolution.

Personalized search results also affect rankings, as well as what results you might get if you replicated the searches I did previously. The engines have long offered users the option to personalize results to some extent.

> The entire nature of search is in a state of constant upheaval and evolution.

For example, some search engines offer the ability to filter out adult content or to only deliver results in the English language.

Say you live in Portland, Maine, and I live in Portland, Oregon. If we both have accounts on Google, MSN, or Yahoo! (e-mail, personalized home pages, maps, photo sharing, document creation and editing—the palette is ever-broadening), we're giving those companies and their search engines the opportunity to learn a lot about us based on our habits, history, and personal (but, it's important to point out, non-personally identifiable) data. So hypothetically, when we both search for the same products and services, your results will be skewed toward businesses in Maine, while mine will land squarely in Oregon. You're a musician; I'm into fishing. So your search for "bass" shows results heavier on musical instruments, whereas my search reveals options for fishing trips, rods and reels, and maybe even seafood recipes.

Your kiwi is a fruit. Mine is a friend from New Zealand where natives are referred to as "kiwis."

Otherwise put, your number-one search result might not even show up in my search results.

Clicking on search result options such as "Similar pages" and "Note this" on Google provide even more personalized results, immediately as well as for similar searches in the future, presumably.

At present, Google is delivering personalized search results to logged-in users, and will likely intensify and refine their efforts in this direction in the future. Yahoo! and Ask are said to be collecting the data that can enable this functionality, but aren't yet serving up personalized results. Given that Google is the 900-pound gorilla of search, personalized search, as well as universal search, matters—a lot.

Personalized and universal search affect SEO, and will only have a bigger impact in the future. Optimization is rapidly becoming more customized and less of a one-size-fits-all-website solution. Optimizing sites, and site elements for search, will likely become more difficult, but the rewards are potentially greater.

Search engines are becoming ever-better at assessing user intent. The fundamental goals of optimization will not change—getting relevant results in front of the searchers who are raising their hands via search, signaling their intent to find web content that addresses their immediate needs.

Universal and personalized search make the SEO game more complex.

Universal and personalized search make the SEO game more complex. Not to be forgotten, however, is that universal and personalized search make SEO more rewarding both to searchers and to site owners.

TRUTH

34

Blogs are built for SEO

Blogs are highly effective tools that can enhance SEO strategies today as well as over the long term in a broad variety of ways. Working with bloggers, as well as launching and maintaining one or several blogs, are tactics every SEO strategist should consider.

Blog platforms are built for search. Although content, names, tags, links, and all those other good things count, blog platforms have plenty of optimization advantages baked into them from the start. Blog structure and architecture offer a baked-in SEO platform. In fact, many commercial sites—including publishers—have recently started migrating entirely to commercially available blog platforms rather than building their own web properties on more traditional (not to mention much more expensive) content management platforms.

Blog platforms are built for search.

Basically, all blogging software packages are simple content management systems (CMS). Here are a few reasons blogs can be compared to a CMS:

- Blog platforms make it easy to add new pages, while at the same time integrating those pages into a site's navigational structure.

- Blogs and blog posts are naturally search-friendly because they're text-rich and link-rich.

- Blogs and blog posts also logically structure and categorize content.

- In a best-case scenario, blogs are frequently updated.

- The URL structure of blogs is simple and search-friendly.

- Blogs contain very little extraneous HTML code to trip up search engine spiders and crawlers.

- Blogs encourage linking—often, lots of linking. Blogs (and bloggers) tend to include far more outbound links in their content than do "traditional" web properties.

Following are some ways in which blogs should be part of your SEO strategy:

■ **Inbound links:** Because bloggers tend to link so freely to one another as well as to news, social media, and websites, external blogs are a go-to source for inbound links. Inbound links can go to either your website or (more likely and easily) to your own blog. For this reason, PR strategies that take blogs and bloggers into account have become a critical component of communications—and SEO—strategies for companies for which prominence on the Web is critical. Blogs support virtually all forms of media in addition to creating a reasonably steady stream of news and information that will attract, interest, and entice bloggers to mention and link to your own web properties. Readily available and frequently updated image, photo, video, and audio files can further build inbound links.

■ **Internal links:** In addition to creating inbound links to a primary website or property, blogs can discuss topics, products, and services that are buried deep within the recesses of a commercial website. Creating deep links in optimized text can help raise visibility and awareness of long tail (see Truth 40, "Wag the long tail") products, services, and concepts, while at the same time raising their potential search visibility. Blogs can also assist in making an overall domain more crawlable when they reside on that same domain (for example, www.blog.YourSite.com).

■ **RSS:** RSS (discussed more deeply in the following truth) feeds syndicated content to search engines, as well as to other web properties. RSS feeds can help build traffic while at the same time boosting search engine visibility.

■ **Frequent updates:** The more frequently content is updated, the more often search engines send crawlers around to take a look-see at the website. Blog functionality has evolved, but blogs are still primarily considered "web logs" or journals that are frequently updated—often, much more frequently than a traditional website is updated. Blogs help

> The more frequently content is updated, the more often search engines send crawlers around to take a look-see at the website.

get new and topical content out there: into search engines, RSS feeds, and other traffic-generating online channels.

- **Keywords:** A blog can be used as a valuable extension of an overall keyword strategy. Keywords and phrases should be applied to the blog's name, meta tags, description, categories, and content.

- **Structured content:** Blog software platforms encourage the creation of categories so that content resides within hierarchical themes. By all means take advantage of this feature on your own blog, and carefully consider the categories and their naming structure. The clearer the categories, the easier it is for search engines to "understand" and contextualize the content, and thus to rank and display it appropriately in search results.

- **Community:** Blogs encourage participation and interaction not just through linking, but also through features such as comments and trackbacks. Encouraging participation on your own blog, as well as actively participating in others' via posting comments, forum citations, and other types of contextually relevant linking, is a form of PR known as SEO PR. SEO PR works to boost blog visibility both within relevant communities as well as in search engine rankings.

TRUTH

35

RSS feeds "feed" SEO efforts

Like blogs, with which they're closely associated, RSS feeds can bolster SEO efforts both as internal and external tactics. "What's RSS?" I hear you asking. It's not an uncommon question. Although the term is often unfamiliar, a large and growing number of web users subscribe to RSS feeds. They just don't call them by that rather prickly term. Instead, they usually just say that they subscribe to a news feed or a blog.

RSS (which stands for either Rich Site Summary or Really Simple Syndication—take your pick) allows newsreaders and aggregators to scrape headlines, summaries, and links off websites for syndication. RSS has long been used to syndicate news content and financial information such as stock quotes. More recently, it's become almost standard operating procedure for blogs. Organizations are turning to RSS to issue events listings, project updates, and corporate announcements. There are RSS feeds that can track eBay listings, products on Amazon, packages sent via major courier services, project management activities, forum and listserv posts, recently added downloads, search results, a book's revision history—you name it.

If it's online, and particularly if it's frequently updated, it's almost certainly "RSS-able." Think of RSS as a way to cull just the information you want from the millions and millions of new pieces of information added to the Web each day.

Best of all, RSS is dead-simple to implement. Feeds are baked into blog platforms, and are well within your developer's reach if you run a more sophisticated site.

Text isn't the only thing that can be fed through an RSS feed.

> If it's online, and particularly if it's frequently updated, it's almost certainly "RSS-able."

Podcasts and videocasts are RSS feeds. Photos and images are easy to syndicate, too, either on their own or within text (think news articles or blog posts, for starters). Pretty much any type of online content can be turned into an RSS feed, a tactic that's particularly appropriate for anything that's updated with any frequency.

So, how can feeds "feed" search engine optimization?

First, consider adding relevant, customized RSS feeds to your own site to provide a steady stream of fresh content to attract search engine spiders and crawlers. We know that fresh, continually updated content attracts crawlers to web pages. It's important to bear in mind that RSS feeds provide links to already extant content that resides elsewhere on the Web, so in a sense it's duplicate content—that is, feeds can't be considered a magic bullet that absolve site owners from the responsibility of creating their own original content. There are a number of things you should consider when implementing RSS into your SEO strategy, as follows:

- It's easy to create custom RSS feeds for targeted keywords and phrases. Google, MSN, and Yahoo! News all offer feeds of search results. News and blog feeds, given the frequency with which they're updated, are an obvious solution for many site owners. A clothing retailer might provide links to fashion-related news, for example, whereas

> ...feeds can't be considered a magic bullet that absolve site owners from the responsibility of creating their own original content.

a lender might add feeds related to interest rates or mortgage news. It's common for sites belonging to public companies to include a feed to current financial news and the company's current stock quote simply by creating a feed linked to a search for their stock market symbol. Privately held companies can create "recent news" feeds on their News or About Us page that link to recent mentions of the company's name, products, or services in the news or on blogs.

- Additionally, services such as NewsIsFree.com build custom RSS feeds from a long and varied list of content provider partners. And don't forget that your own feeds can be fed into different areas of your site. For example, you could create a "new products" or "recent news" feed on your homepage. This tactic can provide deep linking while at the same time encouraging deeper exploration by visitors.

- Like all Web 2.0 social media tactics, RSS is a two-way street where optimization is concerned. Syndicating your own RSS feeds across the Internet can help boost online traffic and increase visibility, as well as give an SEO program a leg up in the process.

- Depending on the types of content you publish, it might be appropriate to create one or several RSS feeds. Each feed should be optimized for search engines—both the major ones as well as specialized blog, news, podcast, and videocast search engines. It should go without saying that feeds should be linked thematically for relevance, which is another reason why some sites might consider syndicating multiple feeds for categories such as news, products, announcements, white papers, research, events, and so on.

- Like an HTML web page, the feed's title is important. It should be descriptive and ideally feature keywords and phrases. RSS feed descriptions are another important feature. These often provide additional information on the site that publishes the feed, encouraging readers to click through for more information on the topic. The titles of each item in the feed are equally important, particularly as each one is a link back to the site publishing the RSS feed. So once again, think keywords.

- Images, such as a corporate logo, help both in branding the feed as well as clearly identifying it for end users.

- Once the number and type of RSS feeds are determined and set up, it's time to take ownership of them and get them "out there." There are a number of RSS feed directories (www.masternewmedia. org/rss/top55/ offers a large list of them) and search engines such as Technorati and Pingomatic. It should come as no surprise that many specialized directories have sprung up for feeds focusing only on realty news, for example, or religious podcasts. Of course, there are podcast and video feed directories, too. As with getting a website listed with relevant directories, registrations help get your content and links out there. Syndication is the name of the game. (A list of some of these directories can be found in Appendix A, "Resources," located online at www.informit.com/ title/9780789738318.)

- The major search engines shouldn't be left out of the feed equation, of course. It's likely that eventually they'll find your feeds, but it doesn't hurt to speed up the process. Add your feed(s) to your own My Yahoo!, MSN, and iGoogle homepages.

- Finally, don't forget to actually subscribe to your own RSS feed(s). It's important to see what end users see, and to stay on top of any technical glitches that might arise.

TRUTH

36

Users will create content for you

User-generated content (UGC) is a powerful SEO tool, and you don't even have to create it. Users do. Studies have found that more than half of web users have reviewed or rated products and services online. And that figure is even higher among "millenials," the 18- to 25-year-old demographic. More than 71 percent of them share their opinions on a wide variety of sites.

We're talking a wide variety of shopping sites, such as epinions, Yahoo! Shopping, BizRate, PriceGrabber, CNET, Bazaarvoice, virtually every travel-related site (such as TripAdvisor.com)...the list goes on and on. Local city guides (Yelp, Citysearch, Yahoo!, and Google Local) are literally filled with user reviews of butchers, bakers, candlestick makers, sushi bars, nightclubs, dentists, and dog groomers. Amazon even encourages its customers not only to rate the products they sell, but also to post their own product photos.

Why so much UGC out there? UGC makes it easy for the owners of shopping, guide, travel, and other product and services-oriented websites to constantly add fresh new content. And users trust it. In study after study, web users who are researching and buying online say they trust the opinions of their peers more than they trust merchants or manufacturers to point their dollars in the right direction. In fact, a UGC Nielsen study found online ratings and reviews are the third most trusted source of marketing, period, following direct word-of-mouth and newspaper ads.

UGC doesn't only exist on review and merchant sites, of course. Wikipedia, Mahalo, and Knol are user-constructed knowledge resources. Flickr, Picasa, and Photobucket accept photos from anyone; YouTube does likewise with video. Any (or all) of these could contain information about your brand, products, or services...and even link back to your site.

Within the context of SEO, it's important to consider a number of factors when it comes to user-generated content, as follows:

...web users who are researching and buying online say they trust the opinions of their peers more than they trust merchants or manufacturers....

- Consider adding UGC to your own site. UGC creates trust and loyalty. It offers visitors deeper information. And it offers you, the site owner, a constantly updated source of fresh content (think spider bait!). You can create community and at the same time boost search engine visibility. There's an extra keyword-related benefit to this type of UGC, too. Users are likely to make spelling mistakes, and even misspell brand and product names. Let them! Common misspellings will help a searcher who's made the same error in a search query land on your site.

- If you go the user-generated content route, make sure the structure of this site section's URLs and templates adhere to basic SEO best practices. Predefine keyword-rich categories, topics, and tags. An additional benefit of UGC is the opportunity to "listen" to consumers discussing you in their terms, which can go far when it comes to keyword strategy. It's also a good idea to come up with ideas to encourage people to post. Contests are always popular (best travel photo, or most unusual place you used this product, for example).

- A drawback of UGC is that it can attract spam or create a need for moderation. The good news is you needn't do it all yourself over time. Reward your most loyal posters with special status. Throw a few perks their way, and confer upon them powers to help keep the community in order.

- Create UGC elsewhere. With sites out there offering user reviews of everything from wine to accountants and college professors, it's likely your product or service has been reviewed somewhere, too. Moreover, there's absolutely nothing stopping you from creating UGC yourself and posting it on relevant sites. Don't go overboard with complimenting yourself, for heaven's sake, but use UGC opportunities to get your name, keywords, optimized images, and multimedia material—and don't forget those all-important links—out there. If users can do it, you can, too.

- Ask your customers and clients to help, too. There are plenty of polite ways to do this, such as a gentle nudge in an e-mail with a link to the appropriate review channel. A hair salon in my neighborhood has a small sign next to the cash register encouraging its clients to review its services on Citysearch, if they're satisfied.

■ Of course, asking customers and clients to review your services or products cuts both ways. Customers aren't satisfied 100 percent of the time, and certainly, reviews can be negative. But bear in mind that unbiased reviews are what lends the review process so much credibility. No one and nothing is perfect for everyone. Users trust reviews precisely because they offer frank and unvarnished opinions. But don't lose too much sleep over a potential negative mention or two. First, it would happen anyway. And second, according to review software provider Bazaarvoice, some 80 percent of all consumer reviews garner 4 or 5 stars. Those numbers alone indicate that the benefits far outweigh the advantages—and that's before SEO even enters the picture.

> Of course, asking customers and clients to review your services or products cuts both ways.

37

Tag images, video, links, and other media

Tags have become a major component of Web 2.0, the iteration of the Internet that actively encourages user involvement and participation. Tags can be associated with text, blog posts, images, video, links, and even entire web pages.

Wikipedia defines tagging as follows: "A tag is a non-hierarchical keyword or term assigned to a piece of information (such as an internet bookmark, digital image, or computer file). This kind of meta data helps describe an item and allows it to be found again by browsing or searching. Tags are chosen informally and personally by the item's creator or by its viewer, depending on the system. On a website in which many users tag many items (such as photo-sharing site Flickr), this collection of tags becomes a folksonomy."

What's a *folksonomy*? It is a collaboratively generated, open-ended system of labeling things. And because tags are user-generated by anyone wanting to label practically anything online (text, photos, video, audio files, and so on), they tend to be informal, somewhat disorganized, and often highly subjective, as well as subject to typos. I might tag an online photo of my pet "Inky." If you didn't know me (or him), you'd be more apt to find it if I tagged the picture as "black cat." Similarly, "apple" might apply to a fruit, or to a personal computer. "Mouse" might be a rodent, or a computer peripheral.

See the similarities between tagging and keyword research? Tags can be viewed as a huge pool of user-generated keywords.

However when accorded a measure of strategic planning and keyword research, tagging can certainly help to boost the visibility of online content. A good example of this is the principal of organized tagging that's been adopted by many conferences, seminars, and similar live events. Such meetings designate an official tag, which is a keyword or phrase participants are invited to use in online discussion of the event such as in blog entries, photos, and presentations. The global Search Engine Strategies Conference, for example, recently asked attendees at their annual San Jose, California, event to tag blog entries, photos, and videos with SESSJ08, so everyone who wanted

Tags can be viewed as a huge pool of user-generated keywords.

to could find material related to the conference, no matter what the material or who posted it.

Search engines can index these "official" tags, which makes relevant materials related to the event searchable in a uniform way.

Blogs, particularly editorial and professional blogs, adopt lists of tags that are assigned to entries. This enables a reader to quickly search for all posts related to a specific name, product, event, service, and so on.

Del.icio.us and furl.net are websites that enable users to "tag" any web page. Del.icio.us describes itself as "a social bookmarks manager" and describes its tags as "one-word descriptors that you can assign to any bookmark." Furl.net calls itself "a free service that saves a personal copy of any page you find on the Web, and lets you find it again instantly by searching your archive of pages. It's your personal Web." Because these social bookmarks and their associated tags are shared with other users of the service, it's not a bad idea to create accounts with del.icio.us and furl.net with the appropriate tags for different pages and elements of a website.

Say your site is about cats. It might have sections about cat behavior, cat health, cat nutrition, kittens, cat toys, cat litter boxes, cat shedding, cat grooming, and cat training. All these pages or sections can be tagged in social bookmark sites such as del.icio.us and furl.net, which can help make them more visible to other users. Similarly, you might post photos of your next corporate event on Flickr or Picasa, tagging them something like "Cat & Co. Conference 2008." You can use other tags as well, of course. Just be sure that you use at least one good, descriptive tag in every post to unify the group. And be objective. Instead of tagging a picture of yourself "me," use your full name, and perhaps your title and company name, too.

In keeping with the social nature of Web 2.0, social sites go well beyond allowing you to tag your own content. Photo-sharing sites enable other users to browse and add their own tags to publicly viewable material, just as YouTube does with video. When developing a list of tags to use on your own content, do some research first. Check out related or categorically similar material on photo-sharing sites, video-sharing sites, social bookmark sites, and certainly in blog search engines such as Technorati. People search engine Spock.com is a good place to research tags related to individuals, running the gamut from company names and job titles to descriptors such as "red hair" and "lived in Paris."

You're likely using tags more often than you realize, both on the Web and on your own personal computer. iTunes, for example, encourages you to add tags such as "rock," "alt country," "comedy," or "audio book" to MP3 files. Gmail invites users to categorize their mail—and hence make it more searchable—by adding tags.

Tags help make digital content more organized and searchable, albeit in the most informal fashion. Tagging is not to be sneezed at for being so unstructured. If tags can help you find your own digital media, they can help lead others to it, too.

Think back to the era of paper file systems. You may have filed your taxes under "income tax 1977" or "IRS 1040 1977." But you tagged that file as something. If you hadn't, you'd never again be able to lay hands on those important tax documents.

If tags can help you find your own digital media, they can help lead others to it, too.

Just as a naming system worked in the era of file cabinets, tagging makes sense for a digital era, as well as for digital search.

TRUTH

38

Being #1 ain't what it used to be

In search engine optimization, the goal is to be the number-one result in organic rankings for a given search term. Right? Or is it? In SEO terms, what exactly does number one mean, anyway?

One recent hot movie is the latest installment in the "Indiana Jones" series. Conduct a search for the term "Indiana Jones," and your mileage will vary depending on when and where you are when you do that search. Is the film in current release? In that case, Google will likely shoot you a link to the movie's trailer and current showtimes in your area. It might give you a box to fill in with your city, state, or zip code to find local theaters. Or if you're signed into your Google account and Google "knows" you're the one who's searching, it might just shoot you the list of showtimes directly.

Are you searching on opening weekend? You might get links to recent reviews on the top of the page, under the heading of "news." You might see a big image of the movie's poster or a still from the film, either in the form of an image file or a clickable YouTube video or the trailer or other material. Google's favoring Wikipedia entries in organic results, so it's likely that the entry for "Indiana Jones" will be high in those organic results.

That same search on Yahoo! displays an organic results page on which the top third of valuable, number-one real estate is occupied with an image linking to the trailer, showtimes, and reviews of the film.

On both Google and Yahoo!, this very relevant site ranks highly, arguably even in the number-one slot. But can it really be argued that it actually ranks as the top organic search result if it's pushed well below the top of the page (where searchers are most likely to see it) by all that other stuff Google and Yahoo! think a searcher looking for "Indiana Jones" might want most to see?

All kinds of things are messing with the concept of being ranked number one, and a rapidly changing and evolving search landscape is going to make the idea of number one murkier, not clearer, in the future.

Universal search

Search results used to be a list of web pages. Universal search now delivers all kinds of results to searchers, culled from the wide variety of vertical content indexed by search engines. Search for a "toaster," for example, and you're likely to see shopping results at the top of the page. Search "global warming," and news stories will probably show up on top of any relevant website dedicated to the topic. Depending on the search, you could get local results, images, video, books, or blog entries on the top quarter or third of the pages, each pushing the "number-one" result further and further down—perhaps to what was once the slot reserved for result #3, #4, or even #5.

The major search engines also develop special results for major events, such as the 2008 Olympics in Beijing. Olympics-related searches display a host of specialized, above-the-fold results.

If universal search doesn't do enough tinkering with "number one," expect to see more havoc wreaked as search gets more personal.

Personalized search

Personalized search features in all the major search engines bring plenty to bear on the elusive number-one results slot. Some elements of personalization are automatic. A searcher in the UK will get primarily English language results, as will a searcher in the United States. But the IP address from which a search is conducted will shunt that search to the U.S. or British version of Yahoo!, Google, or MSN. This can blow a number-one result in one country out of the water (or clear out of the search results, not to mention the number-one slot) for an identical search conducted from either side of the pond.

> If universal search doesn't do enough tinkering with "number one," expect to see more havoc wreaked as search gets more personal.

Searchers are invited to apply filters and preferences to their queries. A searcher may elect, for example, to search within language parameters, or to screen results for adult content. A top news search result might not appear at all in a general web search query.

Then, as alluded to previously, there's the personalized information search engines are able to deliver to users who are signed in to their services, either through an e-mail account (Yahoo! Mail, Gmail, or MSN Mail/Hotmail), or a portal account (My Yahoo!, My Google, and so on). So, Yahoo! may "know" that when you look for queries related to "mouse," you mean rodent, whereas my search history indicates I'm more inclined to seek computer peripheral-related results. With a search appliance installed on a user's computer, such as Google Desktop, personal files related to a query may display over search results.

What's an SEO strategist to do?

All these factors, and more, influence what appears on an organic results page, not to mention what shows up in that coveted and ever more elusive number-one slot. As search evolves into ever-higher levels of technical sophistication, number one will become an even more slippery topic.

Good SEOs are aware of these variables, and aware that much of what determines number one resides well outside their control. Number one is never a realistic search optimization goal because rankings can, do, and will always change. That's why SEO is an ongoing process that aims to position a site or page high in organic search results for relevant searches over a long period of time.

> As search evolves into ever-higher levels of technical sophistication, number one will become an even more slippery topic.

What, after all, is the point in being number one for a day? Or an hour? How high? For how long? SEO is a hugely influencing factor. But ultimately, number one is determined by ever-changing and mutable search engine algorithms.

TRUTH

39

Don't live and die by PageRank

PageRank is named not after how well a website page ranks, but rather after Google co-founder Larry Page. More important, though, PageRank is one of what Google claims are "over 200 signals" its search technology uses to determine the importance, and hence the ranking, of a given web page for a given search term.

Here's how Google describes PageRank:

"PageRank reflects our view of the importance of web pages by considering more than 500 million variables and 2 billion terms. Pages that we believe are important pages receive a higher PageRank and are more likely to appear at the top of the search results.

PageRank also considers the importance of each page that casts a vote, as votes from some pages are considered to have greater value, thus giving the linked page greater value. We have always taken a pragmatic approach to help improve search quality and create useful products, and our technology uses the collective intelligence of the web to determine a page's importance."

Because anyone can download and install a free browser toolbar from Google that displays the PageRank of any page on any site on the Web (on a scale of 1 to 10), many search engine optimizers live and die by that magic number and little green display bar.

Should they? Does PageRank really matter in SEO?

Sort of. Early on in the history of both Google and SEO, it mattered a lot. But PageRank is no longer the be-all, end-all criterion of whether a search optimization endeavor is effective.

For starters, Google has publicly stated that PageRank values are updated only about once every three months or so. Therefore, the value display on that little green

PageRank is no longer the be-all, end-all criterion of whether a search optimization endeavor is effective.

meter is historical, not real-time information. It's also important to bear in mind that the PageRank tool indicates a range—not an exact number—in the "points" it accords a given web page. Even Google reps have stated that PageRank is "for entertainment purposes only," and given the assurances of SEO strategists that the little green bar displayed in the browser toolbar is not the same PageRank value Google uses in real time to determine search rankings.

Google's own GoogleGuide.com, in discussing how to boost PageRank, enumerates a variety of suggestions that mirror the most basic tenets of SEO: Build links, publicize your site, publish RSS feeds, and submit the site to directories and other online listing services. You're doing all that stuff anyway, and you're regularly checking your progress by searching for your site and its associated keywords and phrases on Google, as well as the other search engines. So essentially, PageRank is just one more light on the dashboard, and hardly the most significant one.

Many webmasters and SEOs have long considered PageRank to be the be-all and end-all indicator of whether they should buy a link from another website. The thinking goes like this: The higher the PageRank, the more valuable the link—and the higher the price for buying that link.

Logical, right? Not so fast. Mike Grehan, one of the most respected names in SEO, calls the very notion "ridiculous."

"It's just buying into the myth. A link from a popular and well-visited website can be invaluable if it sends you qualified traffic that converts," Grehan says. "The true value of a link has absolutely nothing whatsoever to do with PageRank."

Don't allow PageRank to become a crutch, or a substitute for more serious SEO initiatives. Sure, it's easy to be seduced by that omnipresent little green bar that rates every web page displayed in your browser. But today, the most seasoned and experienced SEOs don't even have the feature installed. They know it's more of a distraction than a measure of reality.

> Don't allow PageRank to become a crutch, or a substitute for more serious SEO initiatives.

TRUTH

40

Wag the long tail

"The long tail" is a term coined by *Wired* magazine's Chris Anderson to describe the niche strategy of businesses—primarily online businesses—that sell a large number of unique items in relatively small quantities. Think of Amazon.com. Sure, the online retailer profits by selling huge quantities of best sellers, such as the latest Harry Potter installment, to a mass audience. But the company also makes significant profits selling small volumes of much more obscure titles to the much larger group of non-Harry Potter customers. This latter group of products comprise the long tail.

The reason the long tail concept is most applicable to online businesses is that the concept is practically built for search. Why? Well, think in terms of your own site's keywords plotted on a graph. The graph would reach its peak at the most popular term, and trail off gradually for the less popular, more infrequently search terms. Yet the lion's share of the site's traffic, not to mention the bulk of sales or other types of conversions, are likely comprised of these less frequently searched long tail terms.

The reason the long tail concept is most applicable to online businesses is that the concept is practically built for search.

Take an online hardware store, for example. "Hardware" might be the single most popular term used to find the site in search results. But customers who actually intend to purchase "hardware" are few and far between. Actual sales and revenues are generated via searches for "Phillips screwdriver," "spackle," "duct tape," "Allen wrench," and similar long tail terms.

It's not that our hypothetical hardware store doesn't want to rank for the term "hardware," of course, or the name of the business—let's say it's "Acme Hardware Supplies." But from a search optimization perspective, it wants to rank for, and capture traffic from, the hundreds (if not thousands) of infinitely more profitable long tail terms that are its actual revenue drivers.

Optimizing a website for long tail terms requires planning, not only in terms of keywords and phrases, but also site architecture and navigation. Products, information, and keywords should ideally be organized by themes, such as the following:

```
Index: Hardware
        Theme: Hand Tools
                1. Screwdrivers
                        a. Phillips Screwdrivers
                                Brand X Phillips
                                Screwdrivers
                                Brand Y Phillips
                                Screwdrivers
                        b. Battery-Powered
                                Screwdrivers
```

...and so on.

Rich internal linking and breadcrumb navigation helps users and search engines alike burrow into the long tail terms. And on each long tail page, don't neglect the following elements:

- Strong page title

- Highly targeted brief page description

- Short, targeted headlines

- Keyword-rich copy

Does it sound like a lot of trouble to dedicate this much time and attention to each and every small component of your offerings? Well, sites optimize for long tail terms because they're profitable, in no small part because there's so much less competition for them. Let's return to our original example over at Amazon.com. Unless your brand or online presence is of similar size and scale, optimizing for a term such as "harry potter" or "harry potter book" is a formidable challenge indeed. Between the book sites, movie sites, fan sites, and all the other *Harry Potter* content on the Web, you'd be lucky to rank at all. Go down the tail and optimize for something genuinely obscure, though, and you can much more easily find your audience.

The same holds true for paid search, of course. Bidding on terms as competitive as "Harry Potter" or "iPod" can result in a stratospheric cost-per-click. Go down the tail, and you're much more likely to efficiently find an audience for, say, "refurbished iPod Nano."

As a concept, the long tail is easy to understand as it applies to retail websites, but that doesn't mean the concept can't be applied to business-to-business or publisher websites. A solid understanding of long tail terms coupled with a content strategy is key. Perhaps a blog utilizing long tail terms could be part of that strategy. Many firms post white papers and case studies on their websites. These, too, can address long tail terms and attract relevant and highly qualified, self-selected traffic.

And that's the traffic that matters. Moments ago, I searched for "books" on Google. Mighty Amazon.com ranks sixth in organic results, below the fold in my browser window. But when I searched the one-word book title that's currently on my night table—not a bestseller, but a novel by a young and relatively obscure writer—the Amazon results shows up in the number-two slot, just under the book's Wikipedia mention.

> You owe it to yourself to develop a long tail strategy as part of your SEO campaign.

What can your site do or offer that's rare, unusual, specialized, or off-center? What makes your product, service, or offerings unique and distinct from the rest of the pack? The more specific the search, the more highly qualified the searcher, and the further down he is in the purchase funnel.

You owe it to yourself to develop a long tail strategy as part of your SEO campaign.

TRUTH

41

In-house or outsource?

Okay, so you've got an SEO strategy (or at least you're by now beginning to formulate one). It's time to get tactical. But who's going to carry out the ongoing SEO initiative? Do you hire an in-house search specialist, or outsource those duties to an agency, or perhaps to a freelance SEO practitioner?

The answer, of course, is "it depends." A decision is going to be contingent on your marketing budget, the scope of the project (and often, of the websites in question), goals, and whether you plan to focus solely on organic search optimization or will also add paid search advertising or paid performance to the list.

Everyone's situation is different, so let's examine some of the pros and cons of handling search internally versus tasking an outside expert to handle the duties.

In-House: Pros

- SEO is an ongoing process, and regularly updated content goes hand-in-hand with SEO efforts. There can be good reasons to keep all aspects of site management in-house, particularly in industries (such as pharmaceutical) that are strongly regulated, or subject to legal and compliance concerns when it comes to website copy and other site content.

- Many organizations need internal support and champions to get projects off the ground. If marketing, content, and IT are truly in sync and have clearly defined goals, SEO can be effectively managed in-house.

In-House: Cons

- Unless yours is a very small business or site, consider the many duties inherent in SEO. Will one individual (or a small team) be able to optimize multiple pages, write content and tags, build links, and run reports, quickly enough to stay competitive? Ongoing training is practically mandatory to do the job well since the search engine landscape changes so frequently.

- One current and very real drawback is that once trained, SEOs can be extremely difficult to retain. Even in a down economy, demand is high for almost anyone with demonstrated SEO skills in this very nascent marketing discipline. As I once said to a headhunter who called to see if he could pry open my Rolodex, "How many SEO majors did you know in college?"

SEO isn't purely an IT function, nor does it reside squarely within marketing.

- SEO isn't purely an IT function, nor does it reside squarely within marketing. As with other digital marketing initiatives, a solid SEO strategy requires the knowledge, skills, and input of both camps. Ask yourself if your organization is up to that task, and if you can identify an individual who spans these two often-disparate worlds.

- Finally, although costs will be lower than hiring an outside consultant or agency, the burden is high. Assess whether you can support the internal resources.

Outsource: Pros

- An outside agency will have a specialized staff with expertise in the myriad aspects of SEO: strategic planning, copywriting, link building, site architecture, and technical issues. Moreover, SEO is its core competency. It will stay on top of new technology and trends in the business.

- An outside agency or consultant can become a trusted partner that helps keep even the in-house slice of the initiative on track, while offering a fresh, outside perspective on the business.

- Even when in-house personnel are highly competent, driven, and well-compensated marketers, an agency usually brings consistency, continuity, and strategic planning to the table.

Outsource: Cons

- Costs can be considerably higher than running a program in-house.

- Success metrics can result in murkiness and data overload. Even if you outsource, monitoring the success of that effort should be kept in-house, which is still an extra burden of responsibility.

Splitting the balance

Finally, there is one last alternative: Compromise and split the balance. Many companies don't outsource the entirety of their SEO or SEM efforts, but rather those pieces of it they cannot, or don't want to, handle internally. It may be beneficial to work with an agency to develop a long-term organic optimization strategy, but execute most of that plan internally. Alternately, an in-house marketing staff may find that it needs support with only one or two SEO-related issues, which can then be outsourced to an independent consultant. You might, therefore, want to keep the bulk of SEO in-house, but outsource certain specialized tasks, such as overall strategy, site architecture, or link-building.

Obviously, there's never a black and white, right or wrong answer when it comes to hiring any kind of outside business consultant or service. Search engine optimization is certainly no exception. And as search grows, agencies are becoming more specialized. There are now disciplines within search that specialize on local businesses, public relations, multimedia search for audio and video, global and multicultural search, social media search optimization...the list goes on and on.

One person or agency you shouldn't hire under any circumstances: anyone who promises "the number-one slot on Google." There are scammers out there, too. Get references and speak with former clients and employers!

> One person or agency you shouldn't hire under any circumstances: anyone who promises "the number-one slot on Google."

TRUTH

42

Hiring a great search
professional

Whether hiring an outside agency or consultant, or a staff SEO professional, hiring great SEO help begins with knowing what you're shopping for. So, the first step in recruiting the best talent for the job is defining what that job is. You may need SEO help with any—or all—of the following:

- Establishing an overall SEO strategy
- Reviewing and providing recommendations on site content or structure
- Technical advice on site development—for example, hosting, redirects, error pages, or use of JavaScript
- Content development
- Link building
- Managing specific marketing campaigns
- Keyword research
- SEO training

As with any other vendor or employee, check references and speak with current and former clients. Find out what the SEO did, not just in terms of improving rankings, but also in terms of the much more critical areas of helping to improve site traffic, sales, and conversions.

And don't wait to take this step. The time to bring in SEO expertise isn't after a site is built, but as early on in the process as possible to avoid costly mistakes and renovations.

If you're looking to hire in-house staff, it goes without saying that general web literacy is a paramount requisite for the job. Therefore, focus recruiting efforts online, where these individuals live. Sites such as SEMPO, Search Engine Watch, SEO Consultants, and Marketing Pilgrim host SEO job boards. Social networks can also be good resources. Start with LinkedIn, Naymz, and Facebook. Craigslist is another place to look.

> The time to bring in SEO expertise isn't after a site is built, but as early on in the process as possible to avoid costly mistakes and renovations.

Reputable SEO consultancies have high search visibility, not only on the Web, but within their own industry. Their staff and principals frequently write and speak on search, so scan the agendas and speaker biographies at the major search conferences such as Search Engine Strategies, SMX, or Webmaster World. If you're considering hiring an agency or company (rather than an individual), check its affiliations. Does it belong to professional associations that subscribe to codes of ethics and best practices? SEMPO is the Search Engine Marketers Professional Organization, and membership in that body is a vote in their favor.

Online presence counts, too. Does its site rank well in organic search listings? If it can't achieve visibility, it calls into question how well it can do for you or your business.

Is the agency making outlandish promises? Any SEO who claims to have special "tricks" or secret methods to achieve high rankings is lying. There are no tricks to this trade, or secrets. There's just solid knowledge and diligent hard work. Similarly, no one has a "special relationship" with the search engines, or access to Google's "black box." (Believe, me, Google did not become a multi-billion dollar market cap company by sharing the guts or its algorithms with anyone.) Is the company promising to submit your site to "hundreds" or "thousands" of search engines? Nonsense. The ones that really matter are the Big Three, and submission isn't even necessary.

> Any SEO who claims to have special "tricks" or secret methods to achieve high rankings is lying. There are no tricks to this trade, or secrets. There's just solid knowledge and diligent hard work.

Does the agency promise guaranteed ranking? Don't hire them. Instead, run for the door. It should go without saying that the same holds true for spammers. You've gotten those e-mails already, the ones that read:

> "Dear YourBusiness.com,
> I visited your website and noticed that you are not listed in most of the major search engines and directories...."

The best way to hire a great SEO is to learn the basics of SEO yourself, which you're already doing if you're reading this book. Be conversant in the basics and principals of SEO such as keyword research, the role site architecture plays, and the role vertical search might play in your business, for starters.

Google recommends asking the following questions:

- Can you show me examples of your previous work and share some success stories?

- Do you follow the Google Webmaster Guidelines?

- Do you offer any online marketing services to complement your organic search business?

- What kind of results do you expect to see, and in what time frame?

- What's your experience in my industry?

- How long have you been in business?

Finally, beware of black hat practices. Ultimately, you're responsible for your own site. An unethical SEO might deliver short-term results with very long-term—and dire—consequences, such as getting outright banned from the search engines for certain shady practices. And once you're out, it's very, very difficult to get back in. That's something we'll examine more deeply in Part IX, "Don't Be Evil."

> An unethical SEO might deliver short-term results with very long-term—and dire—consequences....

TRUTH

43

Great SEOs sweat the small stuff

Whether in-house or outsourced, you've finally elected someone to head up SEO duties for your website. (Perhaps you're even taking on the job yourself, with or without specialized support.) You've found someone whose skill set marries both marketing savvy and technical expertise.

Now what? What are the SEO's duties, day to day, week to week, and month to month? What should you expect them to do, and how will their performance be benchmarked?

It depends on your needs, of course, but this truth outlines what you should expect functionally from the person (or firm) charged with optimizing your site for search.

Review of site content or structure

The first order of business is a complete site review. The SEO should review a complete outline of the site and its structure, together with a hierarchical listing of every page on the site. If you can't offer this analysis, the SEO should conduct it. The SEO should also review the site's hosting, page redirects, error pages, URL structure, and use of JavaScript.

The source code, programming languages, databases, Flash, content management system, shopping carts, and code validation are all examined and, where appropriate or necessary, tweaked, adjusted, or changed altogether.

Page layout and HTML analysis

In this step, the SEO looks at the site through the eyes of a search engine spider. What part of the site is more important to the crawler? It should be the same elements that matter most to the user, and the site owner. HTML code is also checked for accuracy and syntax. At this stage, the SEO should be able to make specific recommendations regarding page text elements, and source code including the URL, filenames, page titles, descriptions, and meta tags.

Keyword research and analysis

The SEO must then conduct a thorough keyword analysis to reveal which keywords drive the most traffic, and often, which keywords are the most competitive. Less competitive keywords (often, part of the long tail discussed in Truth 40, "Wag the long tail") count a lot. They can still drive a tremendous amount of traffic, and make it easier to optimize specific pages. The SEO should then competitively analyze the websites currently in the top 5 to 10 positions for the top keywords or phrases, paying special attention to those site's structure, page titles, links, page elements, content, and meta tags.

Ranking report

The SEO should deliver a baseline report on the site in question for the targeted keywords. This should reveal where the website ranks for specific keywords on various search engines—at least, the Big Three (Google, Yahoo!, and MSN).

Content analysis and copywriting

The SEO then analyzes web page content. Often, much of it will have to be rewritten, taking into account page placement, keyword density, keyword prominence, and word count.

Link analysis

Links matter, and links relevant to the site's content and site owner's business matter the most. The SEO should examine both internal and external link structures, and come up with a strategy for link building going forward.

> Links matter, and links relevant to the site's content and site owner's business matter the most.

Ongoing monitoring, rank reporting, and recommendations

Using the baseline initial report for each important page, and taking important keywords into consideration, the SEO should monitor the site for performance on at least a monthly basis. These reports not only indicate rankings and search engine status, but also indicate where further performance tweaks are necessary. They can also monitor a site's change in rank relative to search engine algorithm changes, and where a site or its pages stand relative to online competitors and changing user search patterns.

What else?

The preceding list covers the basics, but there are plenty of other tasks that require SEO expertise, depending on a company's needs and the nature of its business and interactive marketing strategy. An SEO can train staff, ranging from webmasters and developers to copywriters, marketing, and PR, in the basics of optimizing a site and its content for search, for example.

It's also not only valuable, but also critical, to get your SEO to take a look at the data generated by your web analytics package. There's an enormous upside in knowing which keywords and phrases are driving users to a specific site or page, and insights that can be gleaned from the actions visitors take once they get there.

> It's also not only valuable, but also critical, to get your SEO to take a look at the data generated by your web analytics package.

There are some additional duties you might also expect from your SEO, or you may even deem some tasks important enough to seek out a practitioner with specific expertise in search optimization. This might include deep knowledge of local search, or search in another geographic area, particularly when foreign languages and search engines are involved. Some search optimizers focus on social media, and others on public relations, optimizing press releases, and online reputation management—that is, how to help "bury" negative citations about you, your company, brand, or products, online.

So what does an SEO do on a day-to-day basis? Plenty. The more you understand what they're working on, the better your communication will be, and the more solid the results.

TRUTH

44

Beware blackhat SEO

Over its brief history, search engine optimization has sometimes gotten a bad rap. Sometimes it's disparaged as a "black art" intended to "manipulate" websites and pages so they'll appear more prominently in search results. The implication is there's some sort of duplicity, malicious intent, or trickery behind these motives.

Well, as long as you're following the guidelines set forth by the search engines themselves, why on earth wouldn't you want to optimize a site to appear high in search results for relevant queries? It's only logical, and it only makes tons of sense, particularly for online businesses, or those hoping to earn money in some way from their web presence.

Then, there's blackhat SEO. And that's a whole other thing. A whole other bad thing. Just as there are unscrupulous plumbers, auto mechanics, landlords, and practitioners from virtually every other industry, there are also, unfortunately, unscrupulous SEOs who fly in the face of Google's well-known "don't be evil" motto.

So in the spirit of caveat emptor, you should know what you're actively not looking for when seeking a search practitioner. We've already looked at a few obvious red flags. You'd never hire an SEO who you met via a piece of spam in your e-mail inbox, nor hire someone who made outlandish promises, such as a number-one position on Google.

In fact, run, don't walk, away from any SEO who promises guaranteed rankings on competitive keywords or phrases. Anyone can get you to rank highly on a wildly obscure phrase no one would ever search— but why would you pay them to do that?

> ...there are also, unfortunately, unscrupulous SEOs who fly in the face of Google's well-known "don't be evil" motto.

A whitehat SEO will be more than willing to explain clearly how he intends to help your site to rank in search engine results, while at the same time ensuring that the site is designed primarily for the end user. That means no deceptive or misleading text. It also means no doorway pages, a frequent blackhat SEO tactic.

Doorway pages (also sometimes called jump pages, gateway pages, or entry pages) are pages designed to show up in search results, but to essentially never be seen by an end user. When that page shows up in search results and a user clicks, they're immediately redirected to the client's web page. Aside from violating the search engines' own guidelines, it's also important to remember that you don't control the doorway page; the unethical SEO does. Tomorrow it could redirect to a competitor's site, or a porn domain. Doorway pages have the potential to be portals to a sort of search engine hell.

> Doorway pages have the potential to be portals to a sort of search engine hell.

Another blackhat technique is cloaking, or creating shadow domains. These techniques differ slightly, but both subscribe to a common tactic: creating keyword-rich sites designed for search engines, but which human eyes will never see. In the end, both techniques reveal one set of content to search engine spiders, and something altogether different to the end user. This violates search engine guidelines, as well as one of the first principles of SEO: Design sites for users, not for search engine spiders.

Finally, follow the money. Your money. You have a right to know where, and for what, an SEO is spending it. Organic search differs greatly from paid search advertising, which is temporary. If you're paying for organic search rankings, don't be deceived by results that appear—temporarily—in the paid search advertising section of a search results page. That's not organic optimization—it's advertising.

TRUTH

45

Search engines frown on keyword stuffing and spam

Several years ago, a friend of mine directed an award-winning documentary film. He paid a guy he'd found on Craigslist to build a website to publicize his project—the film, festivals it played in, his own credentials as a director, and the awards he'd won. My friend had never heard of SEO. He just wanted the site built. The topic of ranking never came up in his conversations with his web guy. The website's background color was white. And on that white background, in white text invisible to the eye, but clear as day to search engine spiders, was the name of the film repeated over, and over, and over again. My guess is the person who built the site had heard of SEO, but knew precious little about it. He was only trying to help. Instead, he came perilously close to getting the site reported to Google as spam and banned altogether.

This is an extreme example of keyword stuffing (not to mention a textbook case of designing a site for search engines rather than end users). It was also a pretty common SEO tactic back in the mid '90s. So common, in fact, that it lead search engines to develop penalties for sites that crammed a ridiculous number of keywords and phrases into website page content and meta tags. Yet people still do it, either by writing copy that repeats keywords so often that the text could not possibly have been designed for actual readers, or by including invisible, and often irrelevant, terms on pages for terms that are frequently searched, such as "sex" or "poker." In the latter instance, these online publishers are trying to drive content to ad-supported pages with popular search terms.

Search engines have developed ways to detect invisible text, whether the white-on-white example cited previously, or text hidden "behind" an image, for example, or buried in CSS coding. Their algorithms have developed to interpret thematic and related ideas and concepts. So if there's 1,500 words of copy on a web page, 1 200 of which are keywords and phrases, that page—and potentially the entire website—will be penalized in search rankings, and potentially even banned from showing up in search results at all. If you're writing real copy for real human readers, this isn't something to lose sleep over, but as a general rule of thumb, keywords and phrases should comprise roughly four to eight percent of copy on any given page.

Keyword stuffing is only the tip of the search engine spam iceberg. Tim Mayer, director of product management for Yahoo! Search, says Yahoo! defines spam as "pages created deliberately to trick the search engine into offering inappropriate, redundant, or poor-quality search results." That's not far off from how the other search engines define the problem, and all offer links to report instances of abuse on their respective sites.

Shari Thurow, an expert in search engine marketing, has identified more than 16 types of search engine spam, or ways people attempt to "fool" the search engines in their quest for optimization. These include the following:

- Keywords unrelated to the site

- Sneaky page redirects

- Keyword stuffing

- Mirror/duplicate content

- Tiny text

- Doorway pages

- Link farms

- Cloaking

- Keyword stacking

- Gibberish

- Hidden text

- Domain spam

- Hidden links

- Mini/micro-sites

- Page swapping (bait and switch)

- Typo spam and cyber-squatting

> Search engines are not public utilities, and are by no means obligated to include you in search results....

The lesson in here for you? Simple. Don't spam the search engines. Ensure that you—or whomever is responsible for building, maintaining, and optimizing your websites—plays by the rules. Google's Webmaster Guidelines are the gold standard in this area.

You can drop precipitously in organic rankings, or drop out of site altogether by being banned from the organic listings.

And if you outsource SEO? Don't be afraid to ask questions, and to clearly state your expectations. Don't forget that search engines are not public utilities, and are by no means obligated to include you in search results if they don't like what you're doing, or if you go out of your way to try to get around their rules and regulations. You can drop precipitously in organic rankings, or drop out of site altogether by being banned from the organic listings.

That's when your headaches will really begin, as explained in the next truth.

46

Don't cultivate link farms

You may remember link farms from the early days of the Web when they were called web rings. Originally, the intention was a good one. Like-minded or thematically related sites linked to one another to help users navigate content on a given topic. Today, a link farm is a group of websites that link to every other site in the network, as well as to external sites, willy-nilly, and regardless of content, context, or relevance. With no degree of editorial selectivity, they're considered a form of search engine spam—the online equivalent of living in a bad neighborhood.

Most link farms display tons and tons of links, with little to no relevant content on the site. The site exists to link for the sole purpose of boosting search visibility. But with no benefit to actual human users, there's no real reason why the link farm should exist in the first place. In fact, most link farms are software-generated, not human-edited. The site's URL is often long and nonsensical, full of keywords and phrases that bear little to no relation to its (nonexistent) content. Often, they reside at domains ending in .info or .biz, as these domains are generally the cheapest to buy.

Google, Yahoo!, and MSN all pay close attention not only to the quantity, but also to the quality of inbound and outbound links. Google's own definition of PageRank specifically states that link relevance (the same thing as link "quality") is accorded more weight than just the link itself.

Nonrelevant links are defined as hypertext links placed on a website or in a directory that have little to no relevance to the linking site or directory. Such links are placed for one of two reasons (or sometimes, a combination of both), as follows:

1. Increasing page rank

2. Getting a website crawled and indexed by search engine spiders

Considering a link? First, ask yourself if the site in question looks human. Does it appear to be well maintained? Is there contact information on the site, either a form or an e-mail address, which can put you in touch with a webmaster? If there's no contact information available anywhere on the site, beware!

If the site in question is a directory, follow a few of the links in the main directory headings. Are the URLs overly long and keyword-stuffed? If you visit one of these sites, does it look pretty much the same as the site you came from? Are there more URLs per page than anyone could reasonably visit?

It's better to miss a linking opportunity than to post a link to your site and get penalized with a drop in your search engine rankings.

If there's even the slightest whiff of suspicion that a site might be a link farm, don't risk it. Stay away. Far away. It's better to miss a linking opportunity than to post a link to your site and get penalized with a drop in your search engine rankings.

The same holds true when you're linking out from your own site. You're known by the company you keep, and if you link to a link farm or other bad neighborhood, you can be penalized as well. Linking to a site is the equivalent of recommending it to your own site visitors, human and search engine spiders alike. Just as you wouldn't knowingly send a friend or colleague to a restaurant that's unsanitary, or in a disreputable part of town, you don't want to send valued traffic into an online netherworld.

Finally, beware of those purveyors of linking software who claim that you can get thousands and thousands of back links to your site with only a click of a mouse and a modest investment. There's only one way to get good, quality, relevant links. Do the research and hand-submit every single link on every single page of your site.

You're known by the company you keep, and if you link to a link farm or other bad neighborhood, you can be penalized as well.

TRUTH

47

It's very difficult to get unbanned

If you, or your search engine optimizer, has been very, very bad, unethical, and violated Webmaster Guidelines, your site can be banned from organic search results. Nobody's going to send you a warning or a telegram when the deed is done. Instead, your site will suddenly just disappear—poof!—from organic results. In short order, web traffic will follow suit.

Getting banned from search engine results turns a website into the proverbial tree falling in the proverbial woods. It's there. But no one can "hear" it. Or, find it, either.

Although outright, full-scale bans are hardly an everyday occurrence, they can and do happen, even to major brands. In 2006, BMW's German sites were banned from Google—which, in turn, resulted in a PR fallout. Doorway pages were the culprit. Nicht gut! The offending pages had been up for a couple of years, but after the company was caught, the sites were gone from Google's results in a couple of minutes—and fully within reason. Google's Webmaster Guidelines clearly state: "If an SEO creates deceptive or misleading content on your behalf, such as doorway pages or 'throwaway' domains, your site could be removed entirely from Google's index."

> Getting banned from search engine results turns a website into the proverbial tree falling in the proverbial woods. It's there. But no one can "hear" it. Or, find it, either.

Sites can be banned for all sorts of reasons, most of them outlined in this section of the book. Whether you were behind the misdeeds that resulted in removal from search results or whether it was an unethical outside SEO who precipitated the ban, getting back in is your problem. You are responsible for a search consultant's actions in the eyes of the search engines.

Getting back in won't be easy. But it's possible, though it's often very time consuming and expensive. The idea, of course, is not to get banned or penalized by the search engines in any way in the first place.

Have you been excommunicated?

If you think you've been banned because your site isn't showing up in search results, the first step is to ensure it really is banned. Try Google first. Go to the search engine and type "site:www.domain.com" and "site:domain.com" (with and without the www; and of course, use the proper suffix, such as .net, .org, and so on). If the result is "Your search - site:www.domain.com - did not match any documents," the site most likely is banned by Google.

If the domain name doesn't appear in search results as a stand-alone domain, or shows up in boldface type on other sites, there's likely a problem with the domain name, with the robots.txt file, or with redirects to the site.

Next, try Google's Webmaster Tools site. A banned site won't show up in the Diagnostics/Web Crawl section, nor will it be visible in the Links/Pages section data. Unless the site is very new and hasn't yet been indexed, or ownership of the domain name has expired, you've likely got a problem. The search engines aren't going to warn you if they find a problem with your site—no e-mail, telegrams, or snail mail. They have absolute and final authority over what sites they include in their indices and what sites they don't. Remember, you don't have an absolute right to appear in search engine results.

Requesting re-inclusion

If you've determined that you do have a problem, review Google's Webmaster Guidelines for potential violations. If you're absolutely certain you haven't broken any of the rules, you can submit a re-inclusion request by signing into your Google Webmaster Tools account. Navigate to the Removed Content tab and click "re-include" next to the content you want to get back into the index. Similarly, you can visit Yahoo!'s Site Explorer and Microsoft's Webmaster Center to determine if a site is in those indices as well.

Now, let's look at the worst-case scenario: You were banned. Now what?

Most likely, you have one shot—one—to get back into Google's good graces. (We'll talk Google here, but this advice applies to all the Big Three search engines.) So, some house cleaning is in order. And that house better be spic and span—absolutely, impeccably meticulous—before you prostrate yourself before Google, hat in hand, and humbly request re-inclusion in their index. When you are ready to send that e-mail, send it to help@google.com with the subject line "Re-inclusion Request."

After that e-mail is sent, be prepared to wait. It could be three months or longer before Google gets to your case in their queue. And when they do get to it, they're going to examine virtually every page of that site with a fine-tooth comb. If they find fault, you're going to go back to the end of that list before you'll be checked again.

This is why the Big Cleanup is so critically important. Not a crumb can remain in even the most remote corner. Sites that are major violators of Google's policies might find that it's easier, faster, and cheaper to rebuild from scratch rather than to seek out and fix every violation of Google's guidelines.

If you rely on search engine traffic for leads, sales, or any sort of revenues, getting banned is a hole you don't want to go into. So stay on the good side of the Webmaster Guidelines!

> If you rely on search engine traffic for leads, sales, or any sort of revenues, getting banned is a hole you don't want to go into.

TRUTH

48

Moving to a new domain is stressful

Just like moving to a new house, moving a website to a new domain is a stress-filled, detail-oriented transition. But sometimes, it just has to happen. Occasionally, circumstances warrant a domain move. Perhaps you've renamed your business, for example, either for branding purposes, or due to a merger or acquisition. Maybe one of your subdomains has swelled in size and warrants a stand-alone website. There are myriad reasons for moving.

When it's time to move, the goal should be to make the experience, work-intensive as it may be for you, friction-free to the end user. In the process, you don't want to leave your hard-earned search reputation in the dust. But do expect a full body-blow where your organic search rankings are concerned, at least until the dust settles.

It will take time for a new domain's pages to laboriously ascend Google's rankings to approximately the same level they previously occupied. On Yahoo! and MSN, the process is sometimes faster. You're likely looking at a one- to three-month gap minimum.

The last thing you want users or search engine spiders to find is the dreaded 404 (file not found) page when they're trying to reach you. That would be the equivalent of moving and leaving no forwarding address.

> You don't want to leave your hard-earned search reputation in the dust. But do expect a full body-blow where your organic search rankings are concerned, at least until the dust settles.

So, let's say you're going to move your domain from www.AcmeDynamite.com to www.AcmeDynamite.org. What to do? Here's what Google's Ríona MacNamara recommends (also see http://googlewebmastercentral.blogspot.com/2008/04/best-practices-when-moving-your-site.html):

- Test the process. First, move the contents of only one directory or subdomain. Then use a permanent 301 redirect to redirect those pages on the old site to the new site. This tells all the search engines that the site has permanently moved.

- Check to see if the pages on the new site appear in organic search results. When you're satisfied the process has worked correctly, proceed to move the rest of the site. Don't do a blanket redirect that sends all the traffic from the old site to the new homepage. Although this will get around 404 errors, it's a bad user experience. A page-to-page redirect (each page on the old site is redirected to the corresponding page on the new site) is more work, but provides users with a consistent, transparent experience. If there isn't a perfect match between pages on the old and new sites, at least try to ensure that every page on the old site redirects to a new page with similar content.

- If you're changing your domain because of site rebranding or redesign, consider doing this in two phases: First, move the site; then launch the redesign. This manages the amount of change users see at any stage in the process, and can make the process seem smoother. Keeping variables to a minimum also makes it easier to troubleshoot unexpected behavior.

- Check both external and internal links to pages on your site. In a perfect world, you'd contact the webmaster of each and every site that links to yours with the request that they update the links to point to the corresponding page on your new domain. Naturally, this isn't possible or practical for sites with thousands, or perhaps even millions, of inbound links. But at least make sure all your own pages with internal links redirect to the new site. Check your web analytics logs for the top-referring external domains and personally contact those sites' webmasters with the request that they update their links to you. Once content is in place on the new server, use link-checking software to catch broken links on your site. This is particularly important if the original content included absolute links (like www.YourDomain.com/music/beatles/sergentpepper.html) instead of relative links (like .../beatles/sergeantpepper.html).

- Retain control of the old site domain for at least three months, just in case.

- Add the new site to your Google Webmaster Tools account and verify your ownership. Create and submit a sitemap that lists the URLs on the new site. This alerts Google that content is now available on the new site and it's ready to be crawled. Don't forget to do the same at Yahoo! Site Submit.

■ Finally, keep both the new and old sites verified in Webmaster Tools. Review crawl errors regularly to ensure that the 301 redirects from the old site work properly and the new site doesn't display unwanted 404 error pages.

Launch the new domain with as much online fanfare as possible: news releases, blog posts, social network updates, banner and search engine ads—as much as time and your budget will allow. The goal is to have, as well as to attract, as many links as possible that point to the new domain to illuminate a path for search engine spiders and crawlers.

TRUTH

49

Global SEO

The Internet isn't hindered by international borders. But the delineations between countries, languages, and even a number of major search engines you've perhaps never even heard of, can trip up even the most solid search engine optimization strategy.

There are plenty of reasons to seriously consider a global SEO strategy, and myriad of considerations within the process itself. You may be doing business across borders and languages, in which case global SEO should be part of your overall marketing strategy from day one. In countries such as Canada, for example, there may be a legal requirement to have both French and English versions of the same website. And no, it won't suffice to simply translate your existing site and hope for the best. There's much more to global SEO than that.

And no, it won't suffice to simply translate your existing site and hope for the best. There's much more to global SEO than that.

Top-level domains

One of the first considerations will be the site's top-level domain name. Some multinational organizations, such as Apple and Microsoft, use subfolders branching out from their top-level domain, each containing a localized version of the top-level, U.S.-based .com site. Other brands, including Google, use country domain extensions, such as .de or .uk. Still other brands use a combination of both strategies.

Which way you go on this may be based as much on technical and business considerations as on search engine optimization. But SEO should play into the decision in terms of how critical it is to capture a certain market or audience via search, and what search engines are dominant in the countries in question. Google, the 900-pound gorilla of search in much of North America, Europe, and Australia, displays country-specific domains with country-specific content in the local language first. So, in the UK, for example, .uk domains are all but guaranteed to dominate search results for any search from a British IP address—unless the searcher consciously changes the default search settings. I certainly wouldn't recommend betting an SEO strategy on searchers doing the work for you.

Where are your web servers located?

Hosting counts, too. A .de site residing on a server with a New York City-based IP address doesn't stand as much of a chance on Google Germany as it would if that server lived in Berlin. Once again, there are other business and technical considerations around this issue, but it's one of the few online instances of physical location making a difference in SEO terms.

Language

Language matters, obviously, as does careful attention to the localization of local languages. This is as necessary for foreign versions of websites as it is for foreign language versions. The UK version of a North American site will sell "holidays," not "vacations," perhaps inclusive of a hired (rather than rental) car. It will offer "mobile phones" rather than "cell phones." There's no getting around the fact you're going to require the help of someone versed in SEO who's perfectly native to the colloquialisms, vernacular, slang, and spellings of the local language.

In search, relevant results are what count, which means content must be relevant to local searchers. This applies not just to the literal translation of the words on a given page, but to their cultural context. Images, video, and other digital assets may need to be re-adapted to an international website, and with them their names, meta data, and other on-page elements that enable optimization. How a given product or service is discussed within a local culture is paramount. How else can a keyword and phrase strategy be developed? What statements and benefits will spur customer conversion? How do locals search, and what are the search trends in their country or region?

Search engines

Once language considerations have been mastered (no mean feat), search engines themselves can often play an enormous role in a global SEO effort, particularly in Asia, where Google (hard as this might be to believe) is an also-ran, as is Yahoo!. In China, Baidu dominates with a 60 percent share of searches. Google exists in China, of course, but primarily for searches conducted in English. If Korea plays a role in your plans, you'll need to familiarize yourself with Naver.

Latin America brings with it another set of issues. Spanish-language localization isn't sufficient to reach Portuguese-speaking Brazil. And even Spanish, of course, is rife with regional variations between the vast expanse separating Tijuana from Tierra del Fuego.

Just as any marketing initiative requires oversight, a global SEO strategy has its own set of specific managerial requirements. In addition to an overall SEO manager, native language speakers who are also local to the individual cultures are a necessity, not an option. Global SEO almost always involves hiring local expertise, often on the ground in the territory in question. It's an investment in time, money, and resources, but one that's worth undertaking for businesses working to reap the benefits of the Web's global reach.

TRUTH

50

Mobile SEO is more important than ever

With more than 40 million users (and counting), the mobile Internet has reached critical mass, according to Nielsen Research. Smart phones, meanwhile, are soaring in popularity. Apple's iPhone is a game-changer, and Blackberries, once reserved for road-warrior high-tech executives, are now commonplace. In fact, 84.8 percent of iPhone users and 58.2 percent of total smart phone users access news and information from their handheld device; whereas 58.6 percent of iPhone users and 37 percent of smart phone users visited a search engine on their phones (mMetrics).

Used to be that mobile sites had to be technically constructed for the mobile channel and reside on special mobile-only .mobi domains. But that's changing. Smart phones may have smaller screens, but they now boast "real" web browsers. (In the case of the iPhone, they use Safari, the same browser that's bundled with full-size Macintosh computers.) The screen might be smaller (Okay, much smaller), but much of the technical heavy-lifting has been eased.

That's because Google and Yahoo! now transcode (a "webby" term coined to define the process of translating digital content from one device to another) the websites mobile users find in search results on-the-fly, and presents (at least in theory) versions of those sites that are visually optimized for the mobile device that did the searching when a user clicked on a search result. So technically, if your already-optimized site looks good on a variety of mobile devices when you arrive on it from a mobile search result, you should be good to go. But be aware that transcoding works only through search. So, the user experience is harder to control on mobile platforms.

> Apple's iPhone is a game-changer, and Blackberries, once reserved for road-warrior high-tech executives, are now commonplace.

Both Google and Yahoo! enable you to submit a mobile site to be spidered by their mobile crawlers. Before doing so, have your webmaster validate that the code is 100 percent XHTML-compatible. Mobile spiders have more trouble understanding invalid code than do their more traditional counterparts.

Having done that, stick with SEO basics: major keywords in the title tag, H1s and body copy, keyword-rich anchor text for internal links, as well as both out- and inbound links. But keep mobile behavior in mind. Mobile users are more inclined to use shorter search queries due to keypad limitations, so ensure that keywords are optimized for the shortest possible term a searcher might use. If they're hungry, they're more likely to look for "pizza" than "pizzeria," for example.

Sounds easy, right? Well, not so fast. Users have much less patience when it comes to mobile search. Don't expect them to go past page two of search results. And with Google only displaying five results on a mobile search engine results page, those two pages display only 10 results. With that kind of competition, mobile search is going to become much more fiercely competitive than web SEO for top-ranked search results.

> ...mobile search is going to become much more fiercely competitive than web SEO for top-ranked search results.

When it comes to the mobile Web, user experience and usability are everything. Screens are small; users are on the go and want results—fast. If mobile search and mobile web users matter to your organization (and mobile is increasingly important for local businesses when people are looking for a theater, restaurant, or drug store), you might have to consider extra measures to make the site more mobile-friendly. This holds particularly true for sites that don't render well in transcoded versions from Google and Yahoo! searches.

In those cases, you have three options:

- **Create mobile-only pages**—Create mobile-specific pages for designated portions of your website. The pages will be narrower, have less functionality, contain smaller images, and will have navigation adapted for mobile users. With this approach, all that's necessary is to update code that already exists. The drawback is that the site's homepage will likely have to work on mobile browsers, or alternately, an extra click will be required to get from the traditional home page to the mobile one.

- **Create a mobile/traditional hybrid**—This model calls for one set of site content (unlike the mobile-only pages option, which duplicates content), but at least two sets of CSS: one for PCs, and an alternate mobile version. In fact, you can build multiple versions of CSS to accommodate different mobile browsers. Each is automatically pulled by an appropriate browser. This approach eliminates the duplicate content problem, but it's not going to be 100 percent reliable. Mobile devices just can't be counted on to select the right style sheet all of the time.

- **Use dynamic mobile pages**—This is the most foolproof—as well as the most costly—alternative. Pay a programmer or developer to combine your content database with a user agent detection to transcode the site on-the-fly. In addition to the cost and work levels involved, it's a short-term solution, due to continually changing mobile technology. But this is your best bet if you want to offer users the best possible experience and also bake the highest level of SEO into a mobile site.

TRUTH

51

Sometimes you don't want to be found

Search engine optimization is the art and the science of making websites—and the content on those sites—visible and accessible to search engines and to searchers. That's not always a good thing. Sometimes, you don't want to be found. What then?

Meet robots.txt.

Think of robots.txt as a spider barrier. The robot exclusion standard, also known as the Robots Exclusion Protocol or robots.txt protocol, is a convention to prevent most species of web spiders and other robots from accessing all or part of a website.

Think of robots.txt as a spider barrier.

Adding a robots.txt file to a website means requesting that cooperative robots ignore specific files or directories. There are lots of good reasons for doing so, with privacy being among the top reasons you might not want information to appear in search engine results. Some sites have sections containing content that's irrelevant to the primary function of the site, which would, in turn, skew the relevance of the site in search indices. Many publisher sites have duplicate content in "print this page" functionality. Robots.txt easily eliminates this duplicate content issue, which would otherwise lead to penalization.

If you want to see a robots.txt file in action, go to SiteOfYourChoice.com/robots.txt in your browser. You'll see a list of the directories the site owner is requesting the search engines to ignore.

Websites with multiple subdomains require each subdomain to have its own robots.txt file. If YourSite.com has a robots.txt file but blog.YourSite.com doesn't, the robots.txt file won't apply to the blog.

Generally, site directories such as /cgi-bin/, /wp-admin/, /cart/, /scripts/, and others that might include sensitive data, such as e-mail addresses and phone numbers, are good candidates for robots.txt. But for heaven's sake, be careful. An improperly implemented robots.txt file can stop search engines from indexing the main content of your website. If you're reading this book, that's unlikely to be your goal.

Be careful not to individually list every page you don't want indexed in the robots.txt file—stick to directories. That way, you're not creating a list of files you don't want to be found, making it easy for technically savvy users to zero in on them.

...bear in mind that robots.txt is never a guarantee of privacy.

And bear in mind that robots.txt is never a guarantee of privacy. Some site administrators have applied the protocol in the blithe belief that they're blocking access to specific content from the world and Web at large. Robots.txt is a request to spiders and web robots to ignore information. It's not a shield of darkness and should never be considered—or used—as such.

About the Author

Rebecca Lieb is a digital content and SEO consultant, as well as a writer, author, and editor. For almost eight years, she was Vice President and Editor-in-Chief of the ClickZ Network, the largest source of interactive marketing and advertising news, opinion, commentary, and resources in the world, online or off. She has held executive marketing and communications positions at strategic e-services consultancies, and worked in the same capacity for global entertainment and media companies, including Universal Television & Networks Group (formerly USA Networks International) and Bertelsmann's German network, RTL Television. As a journalist, Rebecca has written on media for numerous publications, including *The New York Times* and *The Wall Street Journal*, and spent five years as *Variety's* Berlin-based German/Eastern European bureau chief. Until recently, she was a member of the graduate faculty at New York University's Center for Publishing, where she also served on the Electronic Publishing Advisory Group. She frequently speaks on interactive marketing, advertising, and search worldwide.

Dedication

For most of the past 10 years, I've had the privilege of working with, and learning from, the wisest, greatest, and most pioneering, as well as the most generous, minds in search. This book is dedicated to all the searchers: Danny, Mike, Frederick, all the Kevins, Dana, Anne, Amanda, Rand, Matt, Li, Lee, Chris, Frank, Christine, Shari, Brian, Bryan, Chris, Jeffrey, Mauro, Maurizio, Andrew, Elisabeth, Heather, Detlev, Barbara, Jennifer, Jenn, Jessie, Jill, Misty, Vanessa, Sara, David, Mona, and a host of others.

But mostly, it's dedicated to my father, Warren Lieb, who instilled in me the love of searching, learning, teaching, and sharing.

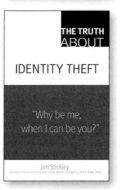